# BEYOND THE BELL

*Reclaiming Emotional Leadership in Schools*

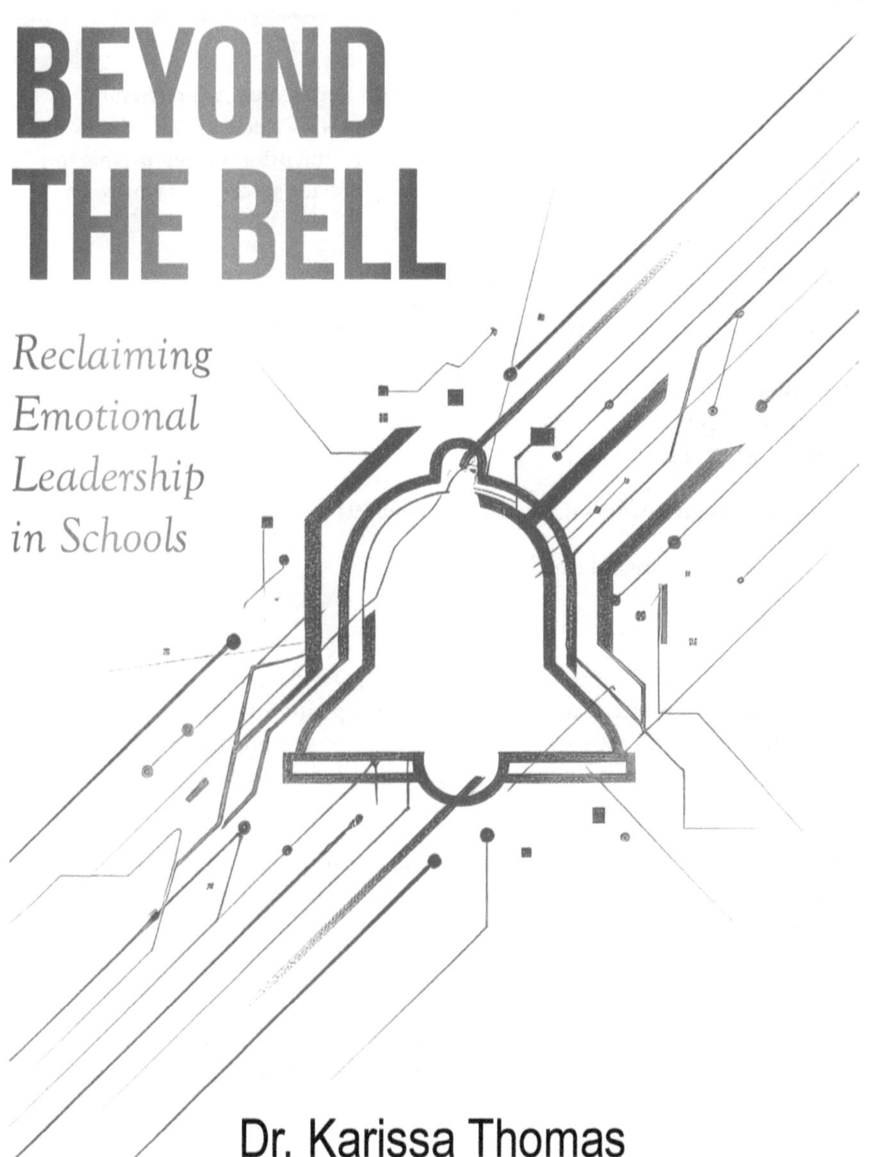

Dr. Karissa Thomas

**Disclaimer**

This book is intended for educational and informational purposes only. It is not intended as legal, medical, psychological, or therapeutic advice. While the author draws on professional experience and research-informed practice, readers are encouraged to exercise independent judgment and seek appropriate professional guidance when necessary.

Any references to individuals, schools, districts, institutions, or organizations are illustrative and anonymized unless otherwise noted. Any resemblance to actual persons or entities is coincidental.

**Trademarks**

The Mosaic Intelligence Method™ and Lead Anyway™ are trademarks of Dr. Karissa Thomas. All other trademarks referenced in this book are the property of their respective owners.

**Bulk Sales and Institutional Use**

For bulk purchases, institutional licensing, leadership development programs, or professional training use, please contact the author through official channels.

To my mother, **Kathleen V. Thomas**—

whose unwavering commitment to education has spanned more than twenty years, and whose quiet strength, consistency, and care shaped my understanding of what it truly means to serve.

You modeled endurance without bitterness, professionalism without self-erasure, and leadership rooted in responsibility rather than recognition.

This book carries your influence on every page.

And to my colleagues and friends who are educators—

those in classrooms, offices, hallways, and communities—

we see you.

We see the long hours, the emotional labor, the unseen preparation,

and the relentless striving to do right by students

in systems that often ask too much.

This book is for you.

# TABLE OF CONTENTS

# PREFACE

## WHY THIS BOOK, WHY NOW

This book was not written in response to a single crisis. It was written in response to a pattern.

Across schools, districts, universities, and national education systems, leaders are being asked to take on more than their roles were ever designed to hold. Expectations continue to expand, resources remain uneven, and the emotional weight of leadership is rarely acknowledged. Leaders are expected to stabilize systems that are themselves unstable—quietly, competently, and without visible strain.

This challenge is not confined to one country. Around the world, governments and education ministries have committed to ambitious development goals, including the United Nations' Sustainable Development Goal 4, which calls for inclusive, equitable, and high-quality education, along with improved literacy and learning outcomes for children, youth, and adults by 2030. These commitments reflect a global understanding that education systems must do more than transmit knowledge. They must develop human capacity, foster social cohesion, and sustain long-term resilience.

Yet while global policy frameworks emphasize access, performance, and outcomes, far less attention is paid to the emotional and leadership conditions required to sustain those goals. Literacy targets, workforce readiness initiatives, and equity reforms cannot succeed without leaders who are supported, grounded, and structurally protected. Educational transformation depends not only on curriculum and infrastructure but also on the human systems that drive change.

For years, the dominant response to leadership strain has been personal resilience. When leaders struggle, they are encouraged to strengthen themselves rather than examine the systems around them. They are offered strategies to cope, adapt, and endure—often without corresponding changes in organizational design, workload distribution, or institutional support.

This book begins from a different premise.

What educational leaders are experiencing is not a lack of commitment or competence. It is the predictable outcome of systems that have not kept pace with the emotional, cultural, and identity demands of modern leadership—whether in local schools, international networks, or national reform environments.

## The Gap This Book Addresses

Much of the leadership literature in education focuses on what leaders should do: manage change, improve outcomes, implement initiatives, and raise performance. Far less attention is given to what leaders are required to hold—emotionally, relationally, and internally—as they carry this work forward.

This gap has consequences.

When emotional labor remains unnamed, isolation increases.

When identity strain goes unexamined, it becomes corrosive.

When care is treated as optional, sustainability disappears.

*Beyond the Bell* was written to make these realities visible—without dramatizing, minimizing, or personalizing them. It is not a book about coping better inside broken systems. It is a book about leading differently so that systems themselves become more human, more resilient, and better equipped to sustain long-term educational progress.

## Who This Book Is For

This book is for educational leaders who care deeply about their institutions—and are quietly questioning whether the cost of leadership has become too high.

It is for principals and assistant principals navigating relentless complexity.

It is for district leaders balancing policy, politics, and people.

It is for ministry advisors, international school leaders, and regional administrators implementing national and global education priorities.

It is for department chairs, deans, and faculty leaders holding responsibility without adequate authority.

It is for educators stepping into leadership roles without preparation for the emotional weight they inherit.

It is also for leadership preparation programs, coaching cohorts, NGOs, and institutions seeking a sustainability language that does not rely on sacrifice.

This book does not assume leaders are fragile. It assumes they are carrying too much alone.

## What This Book Is—and Is Not

*Beyond the Bell* is not a self-care manual.

It is not a motivational text.

It is not a checklist for fixing people.

It is a leadership book grounded in the reality that emotion, culture, and identity are not "soft" issues. They are structural forces. When leaders ignore them, systems fracture. When leaders address them intentionally, systems stabilize.

This book reframes:

- Burnout as a systemic signal, not an individual failure
- Resistance as information, not defiance
- Equity work as emotionally sequenced leadership, not moral performance
- Leadership identity as adaptive and evolving, not fixed or expendable
- Care as infrastructure, not personality

Throughout these pages, leadership is treated as a relational, emotional, and ethical practice—one that must be intentionally designed for sustainability if it is to endure.

## A Note on Tone and Approach

This book is intentionally restrained. It does not rely on dramatic language or urgency-driven persuasion. The leaders reading this book are already under pressure. What they need is clarity, steadiness, and language that respects their intelligence and lived experience.

The chapters are reflective yet practical, research-informed yet accessible, and applicable across K–12, higher education, and international contexts without flattening important differences. Examples focus on everyday leadership dynamics rather than extraordinary crises, because most leadership strain does not come from dramatic moments—it comes from ordinary days under extraordinary demand.

## How to Read This Book

This book is not meant to be rushed. Leaders may find it most useful to move through one section at a time, returning to chapters as roles evolve or new challenges emerge. Leadership teams may choose to read collectively, using reflection tools to translate insight into practice.

There is no required sequence beyond the structure provided. Emotional leadership is not linear. It deepens through revisiting familiar questions with greater awareness over time.

## An Invitation, Not a Demand

This book does not ask leaders to do more.
It asks leaders to see differently.
To see emotion not as an interruption, but as data.
To see culture not as background, but as a force.
To see identity not as private, but as a leadership capacity.

To see care not as indulgence, but as system design.

The invitation is not to become saviors or martyrs. It is to become steady stewards—of people, of purpose, and of institutions that must remain human in order to remain effective.

Education does not need leaders who can endure broken systems indefinitely. It needs leaders who can reshape what should no longer be accepted.

That is the work this book begins.

And it is work worth doing—together.

Awareness must be translated into practice.

## Note on Global Leadership Spotlights

The Global Leadership Spotlights in this book draw on publicly available education policy frameworks, international development reports, and comparative education research. They are designed to illuminate recurring leadership patterns and system-level dynamics rather than provide exhaustive national case studies.

These global perspectives serve a larger purpose: not only to expand understanding, but to clarify what leadership must respond to in practice.

## Leadership Next Steps
*A Practical Companion to Emotional Leadership*

This book identifies what educational leaders are experiencing — emotionally, relationally, and structurally. It provides language for pressures that are often normalized, privatized, or quietly endured. However, awareness alone does not transform leadership culture.

If schools and institutions are to become sustainable environments for the people who serve within them, leadership must go beyond insight and into deliberate action. Not rushed action. Not performative change. But consistent, grounded leadership shifts that build over time.

Throughout this book, you will find sections called **Leadership Next Steps** at the end of each chapter. These sections are meant to connect reflection and application without simplifying complex leadership work into formulas, checklists, or surface-level solutions.

They are not meant to simplify leadership.

They are meant to stabilize it.

Each Leadership Next Steps section offers focused leadership actions that are:

- Grounded in real leadership behavior rather than abstract theory
- Aligned with emotional integrity and long-term sustainability
- Oriented toward systems, culture, and structural responsibility — not just individual effort
- Adaptable across K–12, higher education, and international education contexts

These steps are deliberately limited. They are not meant to add more to already heavy leadership roles. Instead, they help leaders improve how they direct energy, focus, and responsibility — shifting leadership from reactive endurance to intentional sustainability.

## What These Steps Are — And What They Are Not

Leadership Next Steps are not performance tasks to complete.

They are not compliance tools.

They are not self-care prescriptions disguised as leadership development.

They are not one-size-fits-all solutions.

They are leadership recalibration tools.

Each set of steps encourages leaders to analyze how emotional dynamics, role expectations, communication styles, and institutional structures interact — and how small, targeted leadership adjustments can transform culture, trust, and sustainability over time.

This reflects one of the central arguments of this book:

Leadership sustainability is not achieved by doing more.

It is achieved by leading differently.

When leadership behavior, emotional awareness, and system design align, stress decreases without lowering standards. Stability grows without suppressing human nature. Performance becomes more sustainable because people are no longer expected to carry the system alone.

## How to Use Leadership Next Steps

You may engage with these sections in multiple ways, depending on your leadership context:

- As personal leadership reflection prompts
- As discussion anchors for leadership teams and professional learning communities
- As facilitation tools within leadership development programs
- As recalibration checkpoints during moments of institutional strain, transition, or change

Some leaders might focus on one Leadership Next Step per chapter. Others might revisit these sections often as reference tools during tough times. There is no set pace, order, or schedule.

The goal is not completion.

The goal is alignment — between leadership values, daily behavior, and institutional design.

## A Note on Leadership Growth

Sustainable leadership does not come from dramatic reinvention. It grows through steady, grounded practice—done under pressure, during uncertainty, and on everyday days.

These Leadership Next Steps are intentionally structured to reinforce:

- Emotional steadiness over urgency
- Structural awareness over personal blame

- Collective responsibility over individual sacrifice
- Long-term leadership health over short-term performance optics

As you progress through this book, let these sections encourage reflection rather than push for productivity. Leadership renewal needs space as well as action. It calls for discernment as much as decisiveness.

## An Invitation to Lead Differently

Leadership does not improve because leaders become tougher.

It improves because leaders become clearer, more grounded, and more intentional about how emotional labor, responsibility, and care are distributed across systems.

The Leadership Next Steps included in this book are an invitation to practice leadership that protects identity, sustains people, and strengthens institutions.

Not by carrying more.

But by carrying differently.

## A New Leadership Posture
### From Observer to Dissector

For decades, educational leadership has mainly followed a familiar pattern: observe, evaluate, instruct. Leaders are trained to identify performance gaps, measure outcomes, and prescribe corrective actions. This approach has shaped evaluation systems, professional development programs, and accountability frameworks across schools and districts. It is based on a simple assumption: clarity comes when leaders identify what is wrong and explain how to fix it.

That model works well in stable systems but struggles in unstable ones.

The complexity of modern educational environments—characterized by systemic exhaustion, cultural tensions, shifting mandates, and increasing emotional labor—demands a more sophisticated approach. Leadership can no longer be limited to observation and then issuing directions. It must advance beyond simply assessing performance to include structural understanding.

Leadership should shift from evaluating to disciplined analyzing.

An observer sees what is happening. A dissector explores why it is happening. An observer measures outcomes. A dissector examines conditions. An observer evaluates behavior. A dissector analyzes context—emotional, structural, and cultural. The difference is not semantic. It is structural.

When leaders stay solely in observational mode, they risk reducing people to just output. Growth discussions focus on visible behaviors without exploring the pressures that influence those behaviors. In systems already under constant strain, this approach worsens fatigue instead of alleviating it. It also fosters the quiet belief that improvement is an individual responsibility rather than a shared one shaped by environment, design, and capacity.

Dissection, in contrast, is disciplined curiosity rooted in emotional stability. It involves the willingness to pause amid tension and ask deeper, more specific questions. What emotional weight is present in this moment? What structural pressures are limiting capacity? What cultural expectations are influencing responses? What preparation was— or was not— provided? Where might identity strain be affecting performance?

Dissection does not justify underperformance. It clarifies it. And clarity redistributes responsibility.

This posture reflects emotional honesty—the ability to understand emotional patterns without taking them personally or suppressing them. It requires cultural adaptability—the awareness that behavior is influenced by generational norms, community expectations, institutional history, and the unspoken rules of belonging that operate beneath policies. It also demands identity agility—the discipline to separate the individual from the issue and respond thoughtfully without letting pressure diminish leadership presence.

When leaders analyze deeply rather than just watch, they shift from judgment to discernment, from reacting to thoughtful examination, and from working alone to shared responsibility.

## Leadership as Partnership, Not Position

Much of traditional school leadership culture is based on hierarchy: I assess, you improve.

However, growth in complex systems seldom happens just through evaluation. It happens through partnership.

When leadership is practiced as a partnership rather than a position, the tone of professional dialogue changes. Instead of asking why someone is not performing better, leaders assess whether conditions are enhancing or limiting capacity. Instead of assuming deficiencies, they explore design. Instead of blaming individuals, they analyze patterns across teams, policies, and structures.

Partnership does not diminish standards; it enhances them. It ensures accountability while also assessing whether the organization has offered sufficient clarity, preparation, authority, and structural support.

Most educators are operating at the limit of their current capacity. They manage instructional demands, emotional labor, compliance expectations, relational tensions, and institutional instability every day. If improvement is needed—and it often is—leadership must consider not just the individual, but the entire ecosystem influencing their work.

This is not gentle leadership.

It is a deeper form of leadership.

It replaces blame with structural analysis.

It replaces assumption with disciplined inquiry.

It replaces isolation with collective responsibility.

## The Discipline of Deep Leadership

The shift from observer to dissector requires maturity. It demands emotional stability when pressure increases, structural awareness when systems seem unstable, and clarity of identity when leadership is challenged, criticized, or misunderstood.

Dissection slows reactions. It enhances discernment. It preserves dignity.

In educational systems under constant exhaustion, leadership that only observes and instructs worsens depletion. Leaders become judges of stress instead of creators of sustainability. Teams go along outwardly but disengage internally.

Leadership that dissects and partners develops capacity rather than enforcing compliance.

Directive leadership asks, "What should you do differently?" Dissecting leadership asks, "What is unfolding here, and how can we strengthen the conditions together?"

This shift changes feedback conversations. It reshapes the school culture. It rebuilds trust between administrators and teachers. It enables accountability without humiliation and clarity without damaging professional identity.

If leadership is to stay effective in today's schools, it cannot be solely evaluative. It must consider not only whether someone is performing but also if the system is providing proper support. It must examine not only behavior but also the emotional and structural forces shaping that behavior.

This is the posture needed in systems under stress—not louder leadership, not stricter standards, but grounded, emotionally intelligent, and structurally aware leadership.

Leadership that analyzes complexity instead of just observing it does more than boost performance. It stabilizes culture, redistributes responsibility, and safeguards identity.

And in environments where exhaustion has become normalized, stabilization is essential.

It is the work.

# INTRODUCTION

## TEACHING BEYOND EXHAUSTION: A NEW LEADERSHIP HORIZON

Education has entered a phase where competence alone is no longer sufficient.

For decades, schools and institutions have relied on the professionalism, dedication, and emotional endurance of educators to absorb change, manage complexity, and stabilize systems under strain. Teachers learned to adapt. Leaders learned to endure. Institutions learned — often unconsciously — to treat that endurance as a renewable resource.

It is not.

What we are witnessing across K–12 schools, colleges, universities, international education networks, and national education systems is not a temporary wave of burnout, a generational lack of grit, or a failure of individual coping skills. It is systemic exhaustion — produced by environments that demand sustained emotional effort without providing corresponding structural support, relational repair, or institutional stability.

Educators are not leaving because they cannot teach.

Leaders are not stepping down because they lack skill.

Faculty are not disengaging because they no longer care.

They are exhausted because the emotional weight of the work has quietly outpaced the systems designed to hold it.

This book begins with a necessary reframing: burnout is not an individual problem. It is a leadership and systems problem.

## Burnout Is Not a Personal Deficiency

Much of the current discourse around educator burnout unintentionally shifts responsibility back onto individuals. When exhaustion is framed as a personal issue, the solutions follow predictable paths: improve time management, set firmer boundaries, practice mindfulness, prioritize self-care.

While these strategies may offer temporary relief, they fail to address a deeper truth educators already understand: no amount of breathing exercises can compensate for chronic understaffing, policy whiplash, moral injury, or leadership cultures that mistake emotional suppression for professionalism.

Burnout does not emerge simply from doing too much.

It emerges from carrying too much alone.

Across K–12 and higher education contexts, educators face expanding expectations with diminishing authority, rising accountability without meaningful influence, and increasing emotional labor without structural protection. They are expected to be emotionally present for students while remaining emotionally neutral about policies that directly affect their own well-being. They are required to adapt continuously while pretending that adaptation itself carries no cost.

This produces a distinct form of exhaustion rooted not only in workload, but in identity strain. When educators are forced to fragment themselves to survive the role, burnout is not a failure of resilience. It is evidence that the system has exceeded its human limits.

Leadership, therefore, cannot continue treating burnout as a wellness issue alone. It must be recognized as a structural warning sign — a signal that emotional demands have surpassed institutional support.

## Why "Self-Care" Language Has Failed Educators

The rise of self-care language in education was well-intentioned. It acknowledged emotional labor and recognized that stress has consequences. Over time, however, this language has been stretched beyond its purpose — and in some contexts has become counterproductive.

Self-care was never meant to compensate for institutional neglect.

When schools offer yoga sessions instead of redesigning workload structures, inspirational slogans instead of leadership clarity, or wellness emails instead of staffing solutions, responsibility subtly shifts from system to individual. The message educators receive is not care — it is displacement.

This framing intensifies exhaustion rather than easing it. It promotes silence over honest feedback. It reinforces cultures in which admitting strain is interpreted as weakness rather than as professionalism.

Educators do not need more reminders to hydrate. They need leadership willing to confront how emotional labor is distributed, supported, and protected.

This book does not dismiss personal well-being. It clarifies the distinction: self-care is supportive, not curative. Without emotionally intelligent leadership and structurally humane systems, self-care becomes a temporary patch placed over widening fractures.

## Emotional Leadership Is Not a Soft Skill

One of the most damaging misconceptions in educational leadership is the belief that emotional leadership is a "soft skill" — optional, intuitive, or secondary to real decision-making.

In reality, emotional leadership is among the most technically demanding aspects of leadership.

Emotions already shape schools every day. They influence how change is received, how trust is built or broken, how conflict escalates or resolves, and how people decide whether to stay, disengage, or leave altogether. When emotional dynamics go unaddressed, they do not disappear. They operate beneath the surface, shaping culture without accountability or transparency.

Emotionally grounded leadership is not about unlimited empathy. It is about understanding emotional load — how much individuals and teams are carrying, how that weight accumulates, and how leadership decisions either distribute or concentrate it.

It involves recognizing relational fractures created by rushed communication, inconsistent policy shifts, or unacknowledged harm — and understanding that unresolved fractures eventually become cultural fault lines.

It means attending to identity strain — the quiet erosion that occurs when educators feel increasingly disconnected from who they are, what they value, and why they entered the profession.

This book positions emotional leadership as a structural leadership competency — not an optional add-on, but a foundational element alongside strategy, policy, and operations.

## Teaching Beyond Exhaustion

Teaching beyond exhaustion does not mean asking educators to work harder, stay longer, or sacrifice more. It means leading in ways that interrupt depletion rather than normalize it.

It requires shifting from leadership models that reward endurance to those that prioritize sustainability. It involves designing systems that anticipate emotional impact instead of reacting to emotional fallout. It calls for leadership presence that is grounded, steady, and relationally aware — especially under pressure.

For school leaders, this means shifting from becoming emotional sponges that absorb everything to becoming emotional anchors that provide stability without losing themselves.

For institutions, it requires examining long-standing assumptions about productivity, professionalism, and silence — and asking whether those norms still serve the people on whom the system depends.

Teaching beyond exhaustion is not a retreat from rigor. It is a commitment to human-centered leadership — leadership that recognizes emotional conditions shape instructional quality, organizational trust, and long-term retention more powerfully than any initiative alone.

## One Conversation, Two Contexts: K–12 and Higher Education

Although K–12 schools and higher education institutions differ in structure, governance, and daily rhythms, they share remarkably similar emotional landscapes.

Teachers and faculty alike navigate role overload, generational tension, shifting expectations, political pressure, and increasing demands to perform care without sufficient institutional support.

This book intentionally holds both contexts in conversation — not by flattening their differences, but by highlighting shared leadership realities: emotional load, relational fracture, identity strain, and sustainability under pressure.

By bridging these systems, this work offers a broader leadership lens — one that allows school leaders to learn from institutional complexity and university leaders to learn from relational immediacy.

## A New Leadership Horizon

The future of education will not be shaped solely by curriculum, technology, or policy reform. It will be shaped by leadership presence — by whether leaders can remain emotionally anchored while navigating sustained complexity and change.

This book does not offer quick fixes or motivational platitudes. It offers a leadership reframing grounded in emotional integrity, cultural awareness, and identity clarity. It challenges leaders to examine not only what they do, but how they hold people while doing it.

Throughout the chapters that follow, you will encounter leadership moments drawn from real professional dynamics, global leadership patterns, emotionally grounded frameworks, and practical tools designed to translate reflection into sustainable daily practice.

Teaching beyond exhaustion is not about surviving systems as they are. It is about leading toward something better — institutions where care is collective, leadership is emotionally literate, and sustainability is intentionally designed.

The pages ahead invite you into that work — not as a savior of broken systems, but as a steady leader willing to confront the emotional realities of education and build cultures capable of holding the people who make learning possible.

## About the "Inside the Classroom" Moments

Throughout this book, you will find short narrative sections titled *Inside the Classroom*. These are not traditional case studies, nor are they fictional stories meant to entertain. They are composite leadership reflections grounded in real educational environments, designed to surface emotional realities that often remain unspoken.

While this book examines systems, leadership frameworks, and institutional dynamics, these moments return attention to lived experience — what occurs in hallways, staff rooms, classrooms, offices, and meetings, where leadership is practiced daily.

Each *Inside the Classroom* moment highlights how leadership decisions shape emotional climate, how culture is experienced rather than declared, and how identity, relationships, and sustainability are influenced by both small interactions and large policy shifts.

You may recognize aspects of your own experience in these moments. That recognition is intentional. Emotional leadership becomes meaningful when it connects to real practice, not abstract theory.

These reflections are not designed to offer simple solutions. They are designed to cultivate awareness — to create space to observe patterns, evaluate impact, and reflect on leadership presence.

Leadership does not occur only in boardrooms or strategic plans. It unfolds in brief conversations, difficult decisions, quiet choices, and everyday interactions. These moments exist to acknowledge that reality.

## About the Leadership Next Steps

Each chapter in this book concludes with a section titled *Leadership Next Steps*. These sections are designed to translate reflection into action without reducing leadership to checklists or quick fixes.

Rather than prescribing rigid solutions, Leadership Next Steps provide focused leadership recalibration tools — practical shifts in awareness, behavior, and system design that support sustainable leadership practice.

They are intentionally structured to help leaders move from personal endurance toward institutional sustainability, from crisis response toward capacity protection, and from individual responsibility toward collective leadership design.

Some readers will use these sections as personal leadership reflection tools. Others will apply them within leadership teams, professional learning communities, coaching environments, or organizational planning processes. There is no required pace or sequence.

The goal is not completion.

The goal is alignment — alignment between leadership intention, emotional responsibility, and the systems leaders are shaping every day.

# PART I
## THE EMOTIONAL WEIGHT OF TODAY'S SCHOOLS

### The Emotional Reality of Modern Educational Leadership

Before leadership can be renewed, the weight it bears must first be acknowledged. Education has always required emotional labor. What has changed is not its existence, but its intensity, duration, and invisibility. Today's schools and postsecondary institutions operate under sustained disruption—policy shifts, public scrutiny, social polarization, staffing shortages, student trauma, enrollment volatility, accreditation demands, and institutional uncertainty—yet are still expected to project steadiness and optimism.

This section begins where many leadership books do not: with the emotional reality of the work as it is actually lived rather than idealized. Across K–12 schools and higher education institutions, a widening gap has emerged between what educators are expected to manage and what systems are in place to support them. Teachers, principals, deans, department chairs, and academic administrators operate in environments that rely heavily on emotional regulation, yet offer few formal structures for distributing or replenishing that load. The result is predictable. Emotional burden becomes privatized. Individuals cope quietly. Leaders endure silently. Institutions continue forward, often mistaking suppressed strain for stability.

## Emotional Load in Postsecondary Leadership

The emotional weight of leadership does not end at the K–12 boundary. In higher education, the burden takes a different—but equally complex—form. Deans, department chairs, program directors, and academic administrators navigate faculty governance structures, enrollment pressures, accreditation cycles, political tensions, and public scrutiny. They are required to constantly negotiate between institutional demands and faculty autonomy, between financial realities and academic values, and between public perception and internal morale.

Like K–12 administrators, postsecondary leaders frequently function as stabilizers without sufficient emotional infrastructure. They absorb conflict, mediate disputes, uphold standards, and translate competing priorities while often operating without direct authority. The emotional leadership patterns discussed throughout this section—fatigue, containment, invisible strain, and identity erosion—apply directly to campus leadership. While the governance structures may differ, the underlying emotional architecture is strikingly similar.

## The Emotional Load No One Trained Leaders to Carry

Most educational leadership programs emphasize compliance, instructional strategy, evaluation systems, and operational management. Very little prepares leaders for the sustained emotional demands that now define the role. Leaders are expected to absorb staff frustration without defensiveness, hold student pain without becoming overwhelmed, navigate community anger without losing clarity, implement unpopular decisions without eroding trust, and model calm while internally managing uncertainty.

This emotional containment is not incidental to leadership. It is embedded within it. Yet because emotional labor is rarely named explicitly, leaders are often left to manage it instinctively and in isolation. When exhaustion occurs, it is frequently interpreted as personal weakness rather than as the natural consequence of unstructured demand.

## Fatigue as Organizational Feedback

One of the most damaging myths in education is that fatigue signals deficiency. In reality, fatigue is information. Leadership fatigue often precedes burnout. It appears as emotional flattening, diminished curiosity, avoidance of necessary tension, disconnection from purpose, or quiet resentment toward initiatives that once inspired commitment.

These are not character flaws. They signal that emotional demand has exceeded structural replenishment. When fatigue is widespread, the issue is not resilience. It is designed. Viewing exhaustion as feedback rather than failure allows leadership to respond with structural adjustments rather than motivational rhetoric.

## The Emotional Underside of School Culture

School culture is often described using aspirational language—collaboration, innovation, excellence, and belonging. What receives less attention is the emotional undercurrent shaping behavior beneath policy and mission statements. Every institution carries unwritten emotional rules that determine which emotions are acceptable, which concerns are labeled resistance, and who is expected to carry more than others.

When these norms go unexamined, they quietly shape behavior more powerfully than strategic plans. Composure becomes currency. Silence becomes professionalism. Emotional dissonance becomes normalized. Over time, the system rewards those who absorb quietly and marginalizes those who articulate strain.

This section does not advocate emotional excess or the abandonment of professional boundaries. It calls for emotional literacy at the leadership level—the capacity to recognize when culture is sustained through suppression rather than trust.

## Why Resilience Alone Is Not Enough

Resilience is valuable, but it has been misapplied as a structural substitute. When resilience becomes the central survival strategy, systems stop examining demand and instead celebrate those who endure it. Endurance becomes virtue. Exhaustion becomes dedication.

This logic is unsustainable. Institutions do not need more resilient individuals. They need systems that reduce the necessity for constant recovery. Resilience, unsupported by relational support and structural care, eventually collapses. Sustainable leadership requires design, not just determination.

## Setting the Foundation for Structural Redesign

The purpose of this first movement is not to diagnose individuals. It is to surface the invisible forces shaping morale, culture, and identity. Leadership cannot be renewed without acknowledging depletion. Culture cannot be strengthened without examining strain. Sustainability cannot be built on narratives that deny emotional truth.

Systemic exhaustion is not a failure of character. It is feedback. When strain is misinterpreted as fragility, leaders respond with encouragement. When strain is understood as architectural misalignment, leaders respond with redesign. Emotional labor that goes unnamed becomes normalized. Responsibility that remains concentrated becomes unsustainable.

Partnership begins at the point of reinterpretation. It begins when leadership shifts from asking who is not coping well enough to asking what must be restructured so that endurance is no longer the primary survival strategy. Before performance stabilizes, the architecture must be examined. When properly interpreted, strain becomes instruction.

## Partnership Lens

Strain is rarely personal; it is structural. What appears as fatigue is often concentrated responsibility. Leadership strengthens when design changes precede correction. Sustainability emerges when systems redistribute what they once required individuals to carry alone.

# CHAPTER 1

## WHAT NO ONE TELLS YOU ABOUT LEADING THROUGH SYSTEMIC EXHAUSTION

### Global Leadership Spotlight

**Country Focus: United States**
**Leading Through Systemic Exhaustion**

Across the United States, school systems are facing a convergence of pressures that have transformed the daily reality of educational leadership. Districts continue to report shortages of educators in high-need subject areas and geographic regions, while student support needs now include academic recovery, mental health services, behavioral interventions, and family engagement. Meanwhile, administrative responsibilities have become more complex, with increased compliance requirements, data reporting obligations, and accountability measures added to already demanding leadership roles.

National education agencies and workforce research organizations have documented increasing leadership turnover and workload stress in the years after the COVID-19 pandemic. Principals and district leaders are often asked to fill staffing gaps, address community concerns, implement changing policy directives, and handle crisis-level student needs—frequently all at once. In many systems, these responsibilities fall on a small leadership team, creating a situation where exhaustion is no longer occasional but a permanent condition.

This context highlights an important leadership truth: systemic exhaustion is rarely caused by weak personal resilience or poor individual performance. More often, it results from organizational structures that force leaders to absorb instability instead of sharing responsibility. When leadership roles are built on constant availability, emotional containment, and crisis management without sufficient institutional support, emotional labor becomes concentrated at the top. Over time, this concentration diminishes decision quality, limits strategic options, and leads to increased leadership burnout.

Sustainable leadership in this environment requires more than wellness initiatives or productivity strategies. It demands an intentional redesign of how work, responsibility, and emotional load are shared across teams. When systems shift from heroic leadership models to distributed, relational, and structurally supported leadership practices, exhaustion becomes more manageable, and leadership continuity becomes achievable.

**Leadership Reflection:**

Where in your organization are leaders being asked to handle systemic strain that should be managed through shared responsibility, policy redesign, or team-based leadership structures?

*This reality is not unique to one country. It reflects a broader truth about modern educational leadership—one that is rarely spoken aloud.*

No one tells you that leadership will eventually require you to stabilize systems that are themselves unstable.

Not in preparation programs.

Not in onboarding sessions.

Not in leadership handbooks or professional development workshops.

Instead, leaders are trained to manage complexity, implement strategy, and guide others through change, assuming the systems they lead will remain fundamentally sound under pressure. What they are rarely prepared for is what happens when instability becomes the norm rather than the exception, when crisis shifts from an interruption to an operating condition, and when leadership is less about vision than about continuous containment.

This is the unspoken truth of educational leadership today: many leaders are not guiding healthy systems through tough times. They are holding fragile systems together under constant strain, often without proper language, recognition, or structural support.

## When Crisis Becomes Normal

A crisis was once understood as a temporary period that demanded extraordinary effort before a return to equilibrium. In today's schools and institutions, crisis has become ambient. It hums in the background of daily operations, shaping decisions, relationships, and expectations long after the original emergency has passed.

Staffing shortages persist. Policy shifts arrive before previous initiatives have stabilized. Community trust fluctuates. Public scrutiny intensifies. Student needs deepen. Resources thin. And just as leaders adapt to one disruption, another follows.

Over time, this rhythm alters leadership itself.

Leaders learn to move quickly, often without reflection. They prioritize immediate stability over long-term coherence. They suppress emotional responses—not because they are unfeeling, but because acknowledging the emotional cost would slow the pace the system now demands.

This is crisis normalization: the point at which leaders stop expecting relief and begin organizing their identity around endurance.

In a normalized crisis, exhaustion is not viewed as a warning sign. It is interpreted as evidence of commitment. Calm under pressure is rewarded—even when that calm is achieved through emotional suppression rather than sustainable regulation. Leaders become skilled at functioning without pause, even as the internal cost quietly accumulates.

What makes crisis normalization particularly dangerous is not its intensity, but its subtlety. Because everyone is struggling, no one feels entitled to name it. Because the work continues, the system appears functional. Because leaders remain outwardly composed, their internal strain remains invisible.

Until it doesn't.

## Decision Fatigue Disguised as Professionalism

Educational leaders make hundreds of decisions each day, many of them emotionally loaded. Which concerns require immediate attention? Which conflicts can wait? Which voices must be prioritized? Which compromises are unavoidable? Which values can be protected—and which will be deferred?

Over time, the large number of these decisions leads to a specific kind of fatigue that is often overlooked: decision fatigue disguised as professionalism.

Leaders are expected to appear steady, rational, and decisive, even when operating in constant ambiguity. They are expected to absorb frustration without becoming reactive, to enforce policies they did not design, and to explain decisions shaped by constraints they cannot change.

In K–12 contexts, this often shows up in the immediacy of daily problem-solving—behavioral crises, parent communication, staffing gaps, compliance demands. In higher education, it emerges through layered governance, competing priorities, prolonged negotiations, and the slow erosion of institutional trust.

In both settings, leaders learn to perform competently even when clarity is scarce.

What is rarely acknowledged is that decision fatigue does not simply reduce efficiency; it erodes discernment. Leaders begin to default to what is safest rather than what is most aligned. They conserve energy by avoiding complexity, delaying difficult conversations, or relying on precedent rather than judgment.

This is not laziness. It is a predictable response to sustained cognitive and emotional overload.

Yet because leadership culture often equates professionalism with emotional neutrality, leaders feel pressure to conceal this fatigue. Admitting uncertainty can feel risky. Acknowledging strain can feel inappropriate. Asking for support can feel like weakness in systems that quietly reward self-sacrifice.

The result is a widening gap between the leader's external composure and internal experience—a gap that, left unaddressed, becomes unsustainable.

## Leadership Moment: The Parking Lot Pause

After dismissal, the principal sat in the driver's seat for twelve minutes without starting the engine. The building was quiet. The parking lot is nearly empty. There was nothing left to respond to, nothing urgent demanding attention—and yet they could not move. Not because the day had been dramatic, but because it had been relentlessly heavy. Discipline referrals, staffing shortages, a tense district call about new compliance expectations—none of it catastrophic, all of it cumulative.

What unsettled them most was not the workload. It was the numbness. The subtle awareness that leadership had begun to feel like performance rather than purpose. They were showing up, managing crises, keeping the system moving—but emotionally, something had gone quiet.

This moment is often mislabeled as burnout. In reality, it is something deeper. It is what happens when leaders are expected to emotionally stabilize systems that offer no structural relief. When endurance becomes the standard of leadership, emotional depletion becomes invisible.

Many administrators experience this pause privately—long before it shows up in metrics, evaluations, or turnover data. It is often the first internal signal that emotional leadership cannot remain an individual burden. It must become a systemic priority.

## The Grief No One Names

Perhaps the most unspoken aspect of systemic exhaustion is grief.

Not dramatic grief. Not the kind that demands ritual or public acknowledgment. But a quieter, more ambiguous grief, the kind that emerges when leaders realize the profession they entered no longer exists in the form they once knew.

Many leaders carry grief for:

- A vision of education that centered learning rather than survival
- A sense of professional autonomy that has steadily diminished
- Relationships strained by policies that force leaders into roles they never wanted
- The loss of joy, creativity, or spaciousness in their work

This grief is rarely recognized because it does not follow a single event. It accumulates slowly, through small concessions, repeated compromises, and moments when leaders catch themselves thinking, *this is not what I imagined it would be.*

In educational cultures that prioritize resilience and adaptability, grief is often misinterpreted as negativity or resistance. Leaders learn to move past it quickly, reframing loss as growth, change as opportunity, and endurance as purpose.

But unacknowledged grief does not disappear. It hardens.

It can manifest as cynicism, emotional detachment, irritability, or quiet disengagement from the very work leaders once found meaningful. It can manifest as reluctance to invest deeply in new initiatives, skepticism toward reform language, or a sense of professional loneliness—even when surrounded by colleagues.

This grief is not a sign that leaders are unsuited for the work. It is evidence that they care deeply enough to feel the loss.

## Leading Systems You Did Not Design

One of the least discussed realities of leadership is this: leaders are often held responsible for systems they did not create and do not fully control.

They inherit policies shaped by political forces, funding models driven by external priorities, and accountability structures that privilege metrics over meaning. They are expected to implement change while maintaining morale, to communicate alignment while navigating misalignment, and to protect people within systems that offer limited protection in return.

Over time, this creates a particular leadership tension: leaders become intermediaries—buffering staff from system pressure while absorbing pressure from above. They translate expectations, manage fallout, and attempt to preserve relational trust within constraints that continuously test it.

When this work is sustained without adequate support, leaders begin to experience role compression. They are no longer just instructional leaders, academic stewards, or institutional guides. They become emotional regulators, conflict mediators, crisis managers, and cultural shock absorbers—often simultaneously.

This expansion of role without expansion of support is a defining feature of systemic exhaustion.

## Why Naming This Matters

This chapter is not meant to discourage leaders or portray education as irreparably broken. It exists to name what has been largely invisible—so that leadership responses can move beyond endurance and toward sustainability.

When systemic exhaustion is unnamed, leaders internalize it. They question their capacity rather than the conditions. They push harder rather than asking different questions. They normalize depletion rather than challenging its causes.

Naming systemic exhaustion is not an act of complaint. It is an act of clarity.

Clarity allows leaders to distinguish between what is theirs to carry and what is not. It creates space for more honest conversations about capacity, priorities, and limits. And it lays the foundation for leadership that is emotionally anchored rather than emotionally eroded.

The upcoming chapters will not require leaders to become endlessly empathetic or emotionally vulnerable. Instead, they will ask leaders to develop emotional literacy, structural awareness, and strategic grounding, enabling them to manage complexity without being overwhelmed by it.

But before that work can begin, the quiet truth must be acknowledged:

Leading through systemic exhaustion is not a personal failure.

It is a signal that leadership itself must evolve.

Only when this reality is named can leaders begin to move—not back to what once was, but forward toward a form of leadership capable of sustaining both people and purpose in the schools and institutions of today.

# INSIDE THE CLASSROOM

## The Bell That Never Really Rings

The final bell rang, and students poured into the hallway, backpacks slung low, voices echoing through the building. A teacher stood in the doorway, offering smiles, gentle reminders, and quiet encouragement. To anyone watching, the day looked complete.

But the work did not end when the bell rang.

After the hallway emptied, the teacher returned to a desk stacked with unfinished grading, unanswered emails, and documentation forms that had accumulated throughout the week. There was no dramatic breakdown. No visible collapse. Just a long exhale and the familiar calculation: What can I finish tonight, and what will have to wait again?

Later that evening, at home, lesson plans were revised between family obligations and personal fatigue. The emotional shift from classroom presence to personal life felt abrupt and unfinished. The teacher did not feel "burned out" in the traditional sense. They still cared deeply about their students. What they felt was stretched — emotionally present for everyone else, quietly depleted for themselves.

This is the unseen space beyond the bell. It is where leadership decisions about workload, staffing, pacing, and emotional expectations quietly settle. It is where endurance becomes accepted, and sustainability is rarely intentionally built.

---

# LEADERSHIP NEXT STEPS —
## Leading Through Systemic Exhaustion

 **Awareness Shift: Redefine Exhaustion as Organizational Feedback**

Treat leadership fatigue as organizational data rather than personal weakness. When exhaustion becomes widespread, persistent, or normalized, it indicates a mismatch between institutional demands and human capacity. Instead of viewing strain as a personal flaw, analyze where systems are overloading leaders through role compression, constant crisis response, or unrealistic expectations for availability.

**Ask yourself:**

Where is exhaustion managed privately rather than addressed structurally?

 **Leadership Behavior Adjustment: Move From Crisis Containment to Capacity Protection**

Adjust leadership approach from constant stabilization to deliberate pacing. This might involve slowing decision-making processes when possible, resisting a culture driven by urgency, and exemplifying boundary-aware leadership. Leaders don't need to absorb instability to demonstrate commitment. Capacity is preserved when leaders focus on what truly needs immediate attention and handle non-critical issues thoughtfully instead of reactively.

This includes modeling behaviors such as:

- Pausing before responding to emotionally charged situations
- Naming capacity limits without defensiveness
- Delegating responsibility instead of centralizing pressure
- Normalizing sustainable leadership rhythms

When leaders model capacity protection, they give permission for a healthier leadership culture to emerge.

 ### Structural or Cultural Reinforcement: Interrupt the Hero Leadership Model

Examine where your institution depends on individual endurance to maintain stability. Hero leadership — where a small group of leaders takes on disproportionate emotional and operational burdens — results in short-term functioning at the cost of long-term sustainability.

Identify one system-level adjustment that redistributes leadership load, such as:

- Expanding shared leadership structures
- Clarifying role boundaries and decision authority
- Redesigning meeting or communication practices to reduce emotional drain
- Creating collective responsibility for crisis response and emotional labor

Sustainable leadership is built when systems are designed to carry pressure — not when individuals are expected to do so indefinitely.

> ## Leadership Anchor: Lead Systems Without Becoming the System
>
> Systemic exhaustion pressures leaders to act as emotional shock absorbers — bearing instability so others don't have to feel it. Sustainable leadership needs a different approach.
>
> Leaders must stay connected to the system without letting the system take over their identity. This means taking responsibility without taking in chaos. Providing steadiness without losing yourself. Staying present without becoming the emotional outlet for structural dysfunction.
>
> Leadership is not shown by how much instability you can withstand. It is demonstrated by how well you create conditions where constant endurance isn't necessary.

## Partnership as Leadership Architecture 

Systemic exhaustion isn't a sign of personal weakness; it's feedback from the structure. When instability persists, endurance ceases to be helpful and becomes a burden. Leadership improves when emotional burdens are shared before depletion alters identity. Sustainable systems distribute what they once expected individual leaders to bear alone.

# CHAPTER 2

## THE HIDDEN EMOTIONAL COSTS OF LEADERSHIP FATIGUE

**Global Leadership Spotlight**

**Country Focus: United Kingdom
Leadership Fatigue and Identity Strain**

Across the United Kingdom, concerns about the sustainability of school leadership have become a national issue. Education workforce reports, union surveys, and government reviews consistently highlight rising headteacher turnover, ongoing workload pressures, and the emotional stress associated with accountability-driven leadership environments. School leaders are often responsible not only for academic results but also for safeguarding, staff well-being, community relations, regulatory compliance, and crisis management—frequently with limited administrative capacity.

In many cases, the growth of leadership roles has outpaced the systems that support them. Expectations for constant availability, quick responses, and emotional regulation have become standard. Over time, this leads to leadership fatigue that goes beyond physical tiredness and turns into identity strain. Leaders start to feel tension between who they are, their values, and what the role requires. The work no longer just tests their capacity; it also affects how they see themselves, their professional boundaries, and their emotional stability.

This pattern highlights a significant leadership risk. When institutional support does not keep pace with role complexity, leaders must rely on personal endurance to meet organizational demands. This approach leads not only to burnout but also to a gradual loss of professional identity, a diminished sense of purpose, and shorter leadership tenure. Effective leadership depends on systems that safeguard identity along with performance by defining clear role boundaries, reallocating responsibilities, and integrating emotional support into organizational structures.

**Leadership Reflection:**

How might leadership expectations in your system be redesigned to protect professional identity while sustaining accountability and performance?

Leadership fatigue is often mistaken for burnout. The two are related, but they are not the same.

Burnout is usually seen as a state of exhaustion where energy, motivation, and capacity decline after prolonged stress. Leadership fatigue, however, is more subtle. It doesn't happen suddenly, nor does it always become obvious. Instead, it develops gradually, slowly eroding a leader's sense of self, clarity, and professional coherence.

Many leaders continue to operate effectively even as this erosion takes place. They meet deadlines, handle crises, attend meetings, and support others. From the outside, they seem steady. From within, something more subtle is happening: the gap between who they are and who they are expected to be grows wider with each passing season.

This chapter explores the emotional mechanisms beneath leadership fatigue—mechanisms that are rarely named, rarely supported, and almost never included in leadership preparation.

## The Emotional Labor of Instructional Leadership

Educational leadership is, at its core, relational work. Whether in a classroom-adjacent role or an academic administrative position, leaders are required to navigate human complexity as much as institutional structure. Every conversation carries emotional content: concern, frustration, hope, fear, disappointment, ambition.

Instructional leaders are expected to:

- Motivate without overwhelming
- Correct without discouraging
- Support without rescuing
- Enforce standards without eroding trust
- Absorb emotion without amplifying it

This is emotional labor—work that requires regulating one's own emotions while managing others' emotional states in service of organizational goals.

What sets leadership emotional labor apart from other types is its direction. Emotions flow inward toward leaders. Staff share their concerns, students express their struggles, families communicate their fears, and institutions voice their demands. Leaders are expected to manage these emotions without expressing them outwardly or allowing them to interfere with their decision-making.

Yet despite its centrality, emotional labor is rarely acknowledged as a leadership competency. It is assumed to be intuitive, inherent, or simply part of the job. As a result, leaders receive little formal guidance on how to manage emotional load ethically, sustainably, or skillfully.

Over time, this unrecognized labor accumulates. Leaders begin to carry emotional residue from conversations long after they end. They replay interactions in their minds, second-guess decisions, and brace themselves for the next emotional exchange. The work continues, but the internal cost rises.

## The Cost of Constant Emotional Containment

Professional leadership often requires emotional containment—the ability to remain composed, grounded, and responsive even when confronted with strong emotion. Containment is not suppression; at its best, it is a stabilizing force that allows others to feel held without being overwhelmed.

The problem arises when containment becomes constant and one-directional.

Leaders are expected to contain frustration without expressing it, to hold grief without processing it publicly, and to remain steady without revealing the effort required to do so. Over time, this creates a pattern of emotional asymmetry: leaders provide regulation for others while receiving little in return.

In K–12 settings, this might involve managing staff morale amid repeated disruptions while handling criticism from various sources. In higher education, it may require navigating ongoing institutional uncertainty, political pressures, or conflicts within shared governance structures, all while maintaining an air of calm authority.

In both contexts, leaders learn to internalize emotional strain as part of their professional identity. They become adept at appearing unshaken—even when they are carrying unresolved tension, disappointment, or loss.

This constant containment has a cost. When emotions are held without release, reflection, or relational processing, they do not disappear. They settle into the body and the psyche, often manifesting as chronic tension, irritability, emotional numbness, or a sense of detachment from the work itself.

Leaders might not recognize this as emotional fatigue. Instead, they might describe feeling "less patient," "less present," or "less connected." What they are experiencing is not a lack of commitment, it's the cumulative effect of emotional exhaustion without recovery.

## Absorbing Stress Without a Framework

One of the most overlooked contributors to leadership fatigue is the simple fact that many leaders are absorbing forms of stress they were never trained to process.

Leadership preparation programs focus on strategy, evaluation, compliance, and communication. They rarely address how to metabolize emotional exposure, differentiate between personal responsibility and systemic pressure, or process the relational fallout of decisions that cannot satisfy all stakeholders.

As a result, leaders often reflexively absorb stress. They internalize frustration from staff, disappointment from students, anger from families, and pressure from governing bodies—often without clear boundaries between what belongs to them and what does not.

This absorption can feel necessary, even virtuous. Leaders may believe that carrying stress protects others, that emotional self-sacrifice is part of effective leadership. Over time, however, this pattern blurs the line between responsibility and self-erasure.

Without a framework for processing stress, leaders may:

- Personalize systemic failures
- Overidentify with outcomes beyond their control
- Feel responsible for morale, they cannot fully influence
- Experience chronic guilt for decisions constrained by external forces

This internalization contributes directly to identity erosion. Leaders begin to question their effectiveness, values, and purpose—not because they are failing, but because they are carrying weight that was never meant to be borne alone.

## When Leadership Becomes Self-Disconnection

The most profound cost of leadership fatigue is not exhaustion—it is disconnection from self.

As emotional labor accumulates and containment becomes habitual, leaders may find themselves operating on autopilot. They perform the role competently, but with diminished emotional presence. Decisions feel heavier. Relationships feel more transactional. The work feels narrower than it once did.

This disconnection often goes unnoticed because leaders remain productive. They meet expectations. They solve problems. They hold others together. Yet internally, they may feel increasingly distant from the values, curiosity, or sense of meaning that once animated their leadership.

This is identity erosion in practice.

It is not dramatic. It does not announce itself as a crisis. It appears quietly, in moments of hesitation, in a reluctance to invest emotionally, in a growing sense that leadership has become something to endure rather than inhabit.

## Why This Must Be Addressed

Leadership fatigue is not an individual failing, nor is it an inevitable cost of responsibility. It is a predictable outcome of systems that rely on emotional labor without naming, supporting, or distributing it.

Addressing leadership fatigue goes beyond just encouraging leaders to rest or step back. It involves redefining emotional labor as a collective organizational duty and providing leaders with the language, structures, and support they need to process what they bear.

This chapter does not suggest that leaders should abandon professionalism or emotional regulation. It suggests that professionalism must evolve—so that emotional containment is balanced by intentional processing, relational support, and structural care.

In the chapters that follow, we will explore how leaders can develop emotional integrity without self-erasure, how systems can distribute emotional load more equitably, and how leadership identity can be preserved—even strengthened—under pressure.

But first, the hidden costs must be named.

Leadership fatigue is not burnout.

It is the slow erosion of identity that occurs when emotional labor goes unseen, unsupported, and unshared.

Recognizing this truth is not a sign of weakness.

It is the beginning of leadership renewal.

# INSIDE THE CLASSROOM

## The Moment After the Meeting

The leadership team meeting ended on time. Action steps were assigned. Everyone nodded in agreement.

As the room emptied, one assistant principal lingered behind. They sat down, opened their laptop, and stared at the screen without typing. The conversation replayed in their mind: budget constraints, staffing shortages, parent complaints, district expectations.

None of the issues was new. What felt new was the weight.

They noticed something unsettling — they no longer felt surprised by stress. It had become expected. Anticipated. Built into the rhythm of leadership.

Later that week, the same leader found themselves less patient with small issues, more emotionally distant in hallway conversations, and quicker to redirect rather than listen. The fatigue was not dramatic. It was gradual. Quiet. Cumulative.

Leadership fatigue rarely announces itself loudly. It manifests in shortened conversations, decreased empathy, delayed follow-up, and emotional withdrawal. It is not a failure of character. Instead, it signals that the emotional load has surpassed sustainable capacity.

# LEADERSHIP NEXT STEPS —
## Leadership Fatigue and Identity Strain

 **Awareness Shift: Recognize Identity Erosion as a Leadership Risk**

Leadership fatigue impacts more than just energy and performance. It slowly alters how leaders perceive themselves, their purpose, and their boundaries at work. When emotional labor is ongoing and overlooked, it leads to identity strain.

Start noticing subtle signs of disconnection — emotional numbness, impatience, decreased curiosity, or a growing sense of detachment from work. These are not signs of personal weakness. They indicate that leadership roles may start to require emotional self-erasure.

**Ask yourself:**

Where has leadership begun to feel like performance rather than purpose?

 **Leadership Behavior Adjustment: Shift From Emotional Containment to Emotional Anchoring**

Many leaders are trained to suppress emotion — to absorb frustration, grief, and conflict in order to keep systems functioning. Over time, this suppression builds up internally and causes emotional imbalance. Sustainable leadership requires anchoring rather than suppression.

Anchoring involves recognizing emotion without taking ownership of it, staying present without absorbing stress, and responding clearly rather than sacrificing emotional needs. Leaders demonstrate anchoring when they:

- Name emotional dynamics without becoming reactive

- Maintain professional boundaries while remaining relationally available
- Slow, emotionally charged conversations instead of rushing to a resolution
- Practice reflection rather than constant emotional output

When leaders anchor rather than absorb, emotional labor becomes collective instead of centralized.

### 3 Structural or Cultural Reinforcement: Make Emotional Labor Visible and Distributed

Identity erosion accelerates when emotional labor stays unseen. When leaders are expected to handle relational stress without acknowledgment, space for processing, or shared responsibility, fatigue becomes accepted and unsustainable.

Identify one structural shift that makes emotional labor more visible and collective, such as:

- Building formal debrief or reflection practices into leadership meetings
- Creating shared protocols for handling emotionally charged situations
- Redesigning leadership roles to prevent chronic emotional overload
- Recognizing relational labor as legitimate leadership work

When emotional labor is acknowledged and shared, leaders are less likely to bear it alone — and more likely to stay professionally balanced.

> ## Leadership Anchor: Protect Identity While Carrying Responsibility
>
> Leadership roles often reward composure while quietly demanding self-effacement. Over time, this leads to leaders who perform well externally but grow increasingly disconnected internally.
>
> Sustainable leadership requires protecting identity alongside performance.
>
> This involves remaining grounded in values, purpose, and professional boundaries, even when dealing with pressure, conflict, and complexity. It also means not confusing emotional suppression with professionalism or endurance with effectiveness.
>
> Leadership is not about fading into the role. It's about leading from a place of wholeness — where responsibility is taken without losing oneself.

## Partnership as Leadership Architecture

Leadership fatigue turns into identity erosion when stress quietly builds within a single role. Maintaining composure might hide fragmentation for a while, but unresolved pressure eventually changes the self. Partnership reveals hidden burdens before they harden into loneliness. Sustainability safeguards both the role and the individual responsible for it.

# CHAPTER 3

## TEACHER RESILIENCE IS NOT ENOUGH: THE LEADERSHIP GAP

### Global Leadership Spotlight

**Country Focus: South Africa**
**Resilience Without Structural Support**

Throughout South Africa, educators and school leaders operate in environments shaped by historic inequality, uneven resource distribution, and ongoing infrastructure challenges. National education reports and international development organizations have recorded disparities in school facilities, access to learning materials, class sizes, and administrative capacity across regions. In many communities, school leaders are expected to fill gaps in funding, staffing, and social services while maintaining academic standards and institutional stability.

Within this context, resilience is often promoted as a key leadership trait. Leaders are urged to adapt, persevere, and innovate despite systemic barriers. While adaptability and dedication are vital leadership qualities, resilience alone cannot replace structural investment. When leadership sustainability is seen mainly as a personal characteristic rather than an organizational duty, emotional labor becomes individualized, and systemic issues remain unaddressed.

This pattern highlights a broader global lesson: resilience language can unintentionally hide structural issues. When systems rely on the endurance of individual leaders rather than on redesigning workload distribution, strengthening infrastructure, and expanding institutional support, leadership fatigue becomes the norm. Sustainable leadership requires shared responsibility, policy alignment, and long-term capacity building rather than ongoing crisis management.

**Leadership Reflection:**

Where in your context has resilience been used to justify enduring conditions that require structural reform, redistribution of resources, or organizational redesign?

Resilience has become one of education's most frequently praised virtues—and one of its most misused.

Originally, resilience described the capacity to recover after disruption. In schools and universities today, it has quietly been repurposed to mean something else entirely: the ability to endure ongoing strain without complaint, interruption, or structural change. What was once a human strength has become an institutional expectation.

This shift matters.

When resilience is highlighted without systemic reform, it acts more as a diversion than support—shifting attention away from the causes of exhaustion and onto the individuals struggling within them.

This chapter challenges a common story in education: that teachers must constantly "bounce back" while the systems around them stay basically the same. It redefines resilience not as an individual quality to be endlessly developed, but as a shared leadership duty—one that needs structural attention, relational responsibility, and cultural clarity.

## How Resilience Became a Substitution for Support

During intense crises, resilience language can be grounding. It recognizes difficulty and affirms human strength. However, when a crisis becomes ongoing, talk of resilience starts to hide more than it shows.

Teachers are praised for adaptability while their workloads expand. Faculty are commended for flexibility while resources contract. Educators are celebrated for "doing more with less" until "less" becomes the permanent condition.

In this context, resilience becomes a substitute for support.

Rather than asking why educators must recover so frequently, institutions focus on how quickly they can return to function. Rather than addressing root causes—staffing shortages, unclear expectations, initiative overload, emotional labor—systems encourage personal coping strategies and celebrate those who persist.

The result is a quiet inversion of responsibility: structural dysfunction is reframed as a personal challenge to overcome.

This pattern is particularly harmful because it disguises itself as support. Educators are told they are strong, capable, and committed. And they are. But strength without relief eventually causes strain, and commitment without protection becomes vulnerability.

## The Bounce-Back Myth

The idea that teachers should simply "bounce back" rests on a flawed assumption: that the conditions producing stress are temporary, isolated, or unavoidable.

In reality, many educators are not recovering from a single disruption. They are navigating ongoing instability—shifting mandates, evolving accountability measures, increased emotional demands from students, heightened public scrutiny, and expanding roles without corresponding authority.

Bounce-back language suggests a return to baseline. But for many educators, baseline no longer exists.

What does it mean to bounce back when class sizes remain high, planning time remains scarce, and emotional labor continues to grow? What does recovery look like when the next initiative arrives before the previous one has settled, and when "normal" has been replaced by constant adaptation?

The bounce-back narrative fails because it ignores the cumulative nature of educational strain. It assumes educators can absorb disruption indefinitely without consequence. It also subtly communicates that fatigue is an individual issue rather than a predictable outcome of systemic design.

## Leadership Moment: The Faculty Meeting That Broke Something Open

The faculty meeting was moving quickly through the agenda when a veteran teacher raised her hand. Her voice was calm, steady, and tired. "I'm exhausted by being told to be resilient," she said. "The system keeps adding weight, and we're expected to just carry it."

The room fell silent.

No one disagreed.

But no one had named it before.

The leader at the front of the room felt the familiar pull to redirect the conversation and protect the schedule. Instead, they paused. They set the agenda aside and asked, "If resilience isn't the answer anymore, what would shared responsibility actually look like here?"

What followed was not a complaint—it was clarity. Teachers discussed workload distribution, unrealistic timelines, and the emotional toll of constant change. That moment transformed the room's culture. The conversation shifted from coping to collective leadership.

This is the difference between managing morale and leading culture. One preserves appearances. The other creates structural change.

## The Leadership Gap in Resilience Discourse

The overreliance on resilience language exposes a deeper leadership gap: the absence of structural responsibility for emotional sustainability.

Leadership plays a decisive role in determining whether resilience becomes regenerative or corrosive. When leaders treat resilience as a personal attribute rather than an organizational outcome, they unintentionally reinforce cultures of self-sacrifice.

This gap appears in multiple ways:

- When initiatives are layered without regard for capacity
- When emotional labor is expected but not acknowledged
- When flexibility is demanded, but boundaries are unsupported
- When wellness is promoted without workload adjustment

In both K–12 and higher education settings, leaders are often constrained by forces beyond their control. Yet leadership influence still matters—particularly in how strain is named, distributed, and responded to within the institution.

Shared responsibility doesn't mean leaders take on everything. It means leaders refuse to blame individuals for systemic stress. It involves recognizing when expectations go beyond capacity and promoting pacing, clarity, and support.

## Resilience as a Collective Condition

True resilience is not located solely within individuals. It is produced by environments that anticipate strain, provide recovery, and distribute responsibility equitably.

Collective resilience emerges when:

- Workloads are designed with human limits in mind
- Emotional labor is recognized and shared

- Communication is transparent during change
- Leaders model boundary-aware commitment
- Systems allow for repair, not just endurance

In such environments, educators do not need to constantly bounce back because they are not being continually knocked down.

Reframing resilience as a collective condition requires leaders to shift their focus from motivating individuals to examining structures. It invites questions that move beyond personal coping:

- What conditions are repeatedly depleting our staff?
- Where are we asking for flexibility without offering stability?
- Who is carrying the emotional weight of this system—and who is protected from it?

These are leadership questions, not wellness ones.

## The Cost of Ignoring the Gap

When resilience is overemphasized and leadership responsibility is underdeveloped, predictable consequences follow.

Educators begin to disengage—not because they lack dedication, but because sustained self-sacrifice becomes untenable. Turnover increases. Institutional memory erodes. The remaining staff are asked to carry more, reinforcing the cycle.

Equally concerning is the impact on culture. When resilience is praised without relief, honesty becomes risky. Educators learn to conceal fatigue to avoid being seen as incapable. Conversations shift from collaboration to survival. Trust erodes quietly, even as productivity appears to continue on the surface.

Leadership gaps don't always appear as an obvious failure. Frequently, they show up as quiet withdrawal—a gradual pullback from innovation, connection, and long-term dedication.

## Toward Responsible Leadership

This chapter does not argue against resilience. It argues against its misuse.

Resilience matters. Adaptability matters. Endurance has a place in professional life. But none of these can substitute for leadership that recognizes its role in shaping conditions, not just managing outcomes.

Responsible leadership understands that asking people to be resilient without addressing what drains them isn't support—it's avoidance. It also sees that leaders often face the same issue, praised for endurance while quietly suffering under heavy expectations.

Reclaiming resilience as a shared responsibility takes courage. It requires leaders to speak honestly about limitations, to challenge narratives that equate sacrifice with virtue, and to create systems that protect those who sustain them.

In the upcoming chapters, we will examine how leadership can move beyond deflection toward emotional integrity—building cultures where resilience is fostered by structure, not by demands placed in isolation.

Teacher resilience is not enough.

Leadership must close the gap.

Only then can schools and institutions move from survival to sustainability.

# INSIDE THE CLASSROOM

## When "Be Resilient" Stops Working

During a professional development session, the facilitator encouraged staff to "stay positive" and "focus on what they could control." Heads nodded politely.

Afterward, two teachers stood near the copy machine. One finally said what both were thinking: "I don't need more positivity. I need fewer responsibilities."

They laughed softly, not because it was funny — but because it felt honest.

The phrase "be resilient" had begun to sound less like encouragement and more like expectation. A reminder that the system would not change, so individuals would have to adapt again.

What they wanted was not permission to quit. They wanted leadership willing to redesign the work, redistribute the load, and acknowledge emotional reality without framing it as weakness.

Resilience, without structural support, eventually becomes another form of pressure.

---

## LEADERSHIP NEXT STEPS — Resilience Without Structural Support

 **Awareness Shift: Reframe Resilience as a Leadership Responsibility**

Resilience is often viewed as a personal quality that educators need to build to handle challenging environments. This perspective subtly shifts responsibility from institutions to individuals. However, sustainable leadership calls for a different approach.

Start viewing resilience as an organizational result, not just an individual skill. When teachers and staff are repeatedly asked to "bounce back" without support, it indicates that systems rely on endurance rather than redesign.

**Ask yourself:**

Where has the language of resilience replaced structural accountability in my organization?

 **Leadership Behavior Adjustment: Move From Motivating Endurance to Designing Relief**

Leaders often respond to stress by promoting positivity, flexibility, and perseverance. While well-meaning, this approach can unintentionally make overload seem normal. Effective leadership shifts from motivating people to endure toward actively reducing what they are asked to carry.

Leaders model this shift when they:

- Prioritize workload clarity over constant adaptability
- Set realistic timelines rather than compressing change
- Reduce initiative stacking and competing demands
- Address emotional labor instead of framing it as attitude or resistance

When leaders prioritize relief over promoting endurance, they send the message that sustainability is more important than appearances.

 ### Structural or Cultural Reinforcement: Build Collective Support Systems

Resilience becomes regenerative only when supported by structure. Without institutional reinforcement, even the most committed educators eventually disengage or leave.

Identify one system-level change that strengthens collective resilience, such as:

- Adjusting workload distribution to protect high-burden roles
- Creating shared leadership teams instead of isolated responsibility
- Building recovery time into professional schedules
- Aligning expectations with actual capacity

When resilience is structurally supported, educators don't have to rely solely on personal coping strategies to navigate their roles.

## Leadership Anchor: Replace Endurance Culture with Sustainable Leadership

Endurance culture rewards those who bear the most without complaint, quietly equating self-sacrifice with professionalism and loyalty. Sustainable leadership challenges this story by shifting the focus from personal survival to institutional responsibility. True leadership strength is not measured by how much pressure people can endure, but by how effectively leaders create environments that protect human capacity while progressing toward goals.

## Partnership as Leadership Architecture

Resilience cannot make up for architectural misalignment. When coping replaces redesign, exhaustion worsens, and morale declines. Partnership shifts the question from "Who must endure?" to "What must change?" Structural responsibility maintains what encouragement alone never will.

# CHAPTER 4

## THE EMOTIONAL UNDERBELLY OF SCHOOL CULTURE

**Global Leadership Spotlight**

**Country Focus: Japan**
**School Culture and Emotional Norms**

Japan's education system is globally recognized for its strong academic results, high student achievement, and institutional stability. However, national education authorities and labor organizations have long acknowledged issues related to teacher workload, long working hours, and the cultural expectation of professional endurance. In many schools, teachers and administrators take on responsibilities beyond teaching, including extracurricular supervision, administrative work, and community engagement, often outside contracted hours.

These conditions are influenced not only by policy but also by deeply ingrained cultural norms. In Japan, professional identity is closely linked to commitment, reliability, and collective responsibility. While these values reinforce organizational cohesion, they can also mask emotional strain. Leaders and educators might hesitate to show fatigue, uncertainty, or emotional overload because they are concerned about preserving group harmony and maintaining professional credibility.

This context highlights a broader leadership truth: culture exists beneath formal structures. What is emotionally allowed, discouraged, or accepted often affects behavior more deeply than written policies. When emotional labor goes unspoken, it becomes invisible and unmanaged. Effective leadership requires focus not just on procedures and performance goals but also on the emotional environment that influences daily interactions, decision-making, and professional identity.

**Leadership Reflection:**

What unspoken emotional expectations influence how people show up, speak up, or remain silent in your institution?

School culture is not what is written.

It is what is felt.

Mission statements, strategic plans, and professional norms present a carefully crafted image of how an institution perceives itself. However, culture is not created through documents or slogans. Instead, it develops through everyday emotional interactions—what is promoted, tolerated, silenced, or quietly absorbed.

In schools and universities alike, culture exists beneath the surface of formal structures. It influences how people present themselves, how much they invest, how honestly they communicate, and how long they remain. While policy may establish expectations, it is emotional norms—often unspoken—that determine whether those expectations are met with engagement or compliance, trust or withdrawal.

This chapter examines the emotional underbelly of school culture: the patterns that rarely appear in reports or surveys, yet exert extraordinary influence over performance, morale, and sustainability.

## Passive Disengagement: When Presence Replaces Commitment

One of the most common—and least discussed—cultural shifts in education today is passive disengagement.

Passive disengagement is not overt resistance. It does not announce itself through conflict or refusal. It appears instead as minimal compliance: showing up, completing required tasks, avoiding risk, and conserving emotional energy. On paper, everything looks functional. In practice, something essential is missing.

Educators who experience passive disengagement may still fulfill expectations, but they no longer exhibit curiosity, creativity, or initiative in their work. Innovation seems unsafe. Extra effort appears unrewarded. Emotional investment feels risky in environments where it is seldom reciprocated.

This form of disengagement often emerges in cultures where:

- Feedback is inconsistent or punitive
- Change is constant but poorly communicated
- Emotional labor is expected but unacknowledged
- Voice is solicited but rarely acted upon

Over time, educators learn to protect themselves by narrowing their contribution. They do not withdraw because they lack professionalism; they withdraw because engagement has become emotionally expensive.

Leaders might see this as complacency or apathy. In fact, it is often a protective reaction to extended uncertainty or unmet relational needs.

## Toxic Positivity: When Optimism Silences Truth

Positivity has long been valued in educational settings. Encouragement matters. Hope matters. Forward-looking leadership matters. But when positivity becomes mandatory—when it crowds out honesty—it turns toxic.

Toxic positivity happens when institutions push optimism at the cost of emotional honesty. Difficult conversations are seen as negative. Valid concerns are dismissed as resistance. Grief, frustration, or exhaustion are downplayed in favor of "focusing on solutions" or "keeping morale high."

This creates a paradoxical culture: one that seems supportive on the outside but discourages authenticity underneath.

Educators quickly learn which emotions are acceptable and which are not. Gratitude is appreciated. Enthusiasm is encouraged. Doubt, fear, or grief are quietly pushed aside. Over time, this emotional filtering distorts communication and erodes trust.

In these environments, leaders might think they're building resilience when they're actually hiding signals. Emotions that can't be openly expressed don't just disappear; they come back in sneaky ways—like sarcasm, disengagement, burnout, or silent resistance.

True optimism is grounded in reality. Toxic positivity avoids it.

## Silent Resistance: What Happens When Voice Feels Unsafe

Not all resistance is loud.

In cultures where honesty in speech carries risks, whether professional, relational, or reputational, resistance often becomes silent. Educators go along outwardly while disengaging internally. They nod during meetings but hold back their insights. They carry out initiatives mechanically, without true belief or investment.

Silent resistance is especially hard for leaders to tackle because it is unseen. There are no official complaints, no loud conflicts. Metrics might stay steady for a while. But beneath the surface, alignment starts to break down.

This form of resistance often develops in response to repeated experiences of:

- Being asked for input without seeing the impact
- Witnessing leadership decisions that contradict stated values

- Feeling emotionally exposed without protection
- Carrying consequences without influence

When educators lose faith that their voice matters—or that it is safe to speak up—they adapt by becoming strategically quiet.

Silence, in this situation, does not mean agreement. It signals that relational trust has been damaged beyond what words alone can fix.

## Emotional Norms: The Invisible Architects of Performance

Every school and institution operates within a set of emotional norms—unwritten rules that govern how people are expected to feel, express, and manage emotion at work.

These norms answer questions such as:

- Which emotions are acceptable to show?
- Who is allowed to express frustration or doubt?
- How quickly must people "move on" from disappointment?
- Whose emotional needs are prioritized—and whose are minimized?

Emotional norms are powerful because they shape behavior without formal enforcement. They influence who speaks up, who takes risks, who seeks support, and who quietly endures.

In cultures where emotional norms favor suppression, performance may appear strong in the short term. People comply. Deadlines are met. But over time, the cost becomes clear: diminished trust, reduced creativity, and increasing attrition.

In cultures where emotional norms allow for honesty without chaos, leaders gain access to vital information. Concerns surface earlier. Conflict becomes navigable rather than explosive. Emotional labor is shared rather than concentrated.

Policy can mandate behavior. Emotional norms determine whether that behavior is sustainable.

## Why Leaders Must Look Beneath the Surface

The emotional core of culture is easy to overlook because it doesn't announce itself. It takes leaders paying attention not only to results but also to the atmosphere. Not just to compliance but also to energy. Not only to what is said but to what is left unsaid.

This is not a call for emotional overexposure or unfiltered expression. Professional boundaries matter. Structure matters. But emotional literacy at the leadership level matters just as much.

Leaders who understand emotional undercurrents are better equipped to:

- Distinguish disengagement from defiance
- Address resistance without escalating conflict
- Foster trust without sacrificing standards
- Design cultures where performance and wellbeing reinforce each other

Ignoring the emotional underbelly does not preserve professionalism; it undermines it.

## Setting the Stage for Cultural Repair

Part I of this book has highlighted realities that are often felt but rarely spoken about: systemic exhaustion, leadership fatigue, misused resilience, and emotionally distorted cultures. These are not isolated problems; they are interconnected signals pointing to the same conclusion: schools cannot maintain excellence through emotional silence alone.

Culture is not repaired through slogans or morale initiatives. It is repaired through leadership willing to engage with emotional truth—carefully, intentionally, and structurally.

The chapters that follow will move from diagnosis to direction. They will explore how leaders can lead with emotional integrity, redistribute emotional load, and rebuild trust without absorbing everything themselves.

But that work begins here—with the willingness to look beneath the surface and acknowledge what culture actually feels like.

Because what is felt, not what is written, determines whether people merely remain—or truly belong.

# INSIDE THE CLASSROOM

## What the Culture Feels Like

A new teacher joined the school midyear. No one said the culture was tense. No one wrote it in a handbook. But it was felt immediately.

Conversations were guarded. Meetings felt rushed. Staff avoided difficult topics. Smiles were polite but distant.

By the end of the first month, the teacher knew which concerns were safe to raise and which should be kept quiet. The culture taught the rules without speaking them.

School culture is not defined by mission statements. It is shaped by what people feel permitted to say, how conflict is handled, and whether emotional honesty is met with support or silence.

What is felt will always matter more than what is written.

---

## LEADERSHIP NEXT STEPS —
## School Culture and Emotional Norms

 **Awareness Shift: Make Emotional Culture Visible**

School culture is not defined only by policies, mission statements, or strategic plans. It is shaped by emotional norms — what people feel allowed to express, suppress, question, or avoid. When these norms go unexamined, they quietly influence behavior, trust, and engagement.

Start observing the emotional patterns in your institution. Notice which emotions are accepted and which are discouraged. Pay attention to where silence happens, where conversations are guarded, and where authenticity feels risky. These patterns are not accidental; they serve as cultural signals.

**Ask yourself:**

What emotional rules operate beneath the surface of our school culture?

### 2  Leadership Behavior Adjustment: Model Emotionally Honest Professionalism

Leaders play a key role in establishing emotional norms. When leaders exhibit defensiveness, urgency, or emotional suppression, these behaviors tend to spread. Conversely, when leaders demonstrate calm honesty, relational stability, and respectful dialogue, psychological safety improves.

Emotionally honest professionalism does not mean oversharing emotions. It involves recognizing reality without exaggeration and fostering an environment where truth can exist without chaos. Leaders demonstrate this by:

- Naming tension without assigning blame
- Inviting honest feedback without punishment
- Responding to emotion with steadiness rather than avoidance
- Addressing conflict directly instead of allowing silent disengagement

When leaders model emotional clarity, they give others permission to engage more fully and authentically.

## 3 Structural or Cultural Reinforcement: Align Systems with Emotional Safety

Culture is reinforced through everyday structures. Meeting norms, communication channels, evaluation practices, and leadership responses all signal what is emotionally safe or unsafe within an institution.

Identify one structural practice that can better support an emotionally healthy culture, such as:

- Creating protected spaces for dialogue and reflection
- Establishing clear conflict-resolution protocols
- Adjusting meeting formats to allow for voice and processing
- Ensuring feedback systems are constructive rather than punitive

When systems reinforce emotional safety, trust becomes sustainable rather than fragile.

## Leadership Anchor: Shape Culture Through What You Normalize

Leaders shape culture less through formal messaging and more through what they consistently tolerate, reward, and model. Emotional norms are embedded not only by policy but also by daily leadership behavior.

Culture changes when leaders interrupt silence, challenge performative positivity, and make space for honest engagement. Sustainable school culture is built when emotional truth is treated as leadership data — not disruption.

# Partnership as Leadership Architecture

What is felt always surpasses what is written. Emotional currents shape culture long before formal language reflects them. Partnership recognizes what systems quietly normalize and redistributes what has been silently carried. Culture stabilizes when emotional labor is acknowledged and shared rather than absorbed in isolation.

## Part I Synthesis

### From Emotional Weight to Shared Responsibility

Part I of this book highlights realities that many educational leaders privately acknowledge but rarely speak about openly. Systemic exhaustion, leadership fatigue, misused resilience, and invisible emotional norms are not separate problems. They are interconnected signs pointing to a deeper leadership issue: modern education systems have increased emotional demands without redesigning the structures meant to distribute and support them.

Across various national and institutional contexts, a clear pattern appears. Leaders are expected to stabilize systems that remain unstable. Educators are encouraged to show resilience without receiving structural support. Emotional labor is silently absorbed, often without recognition. Cultural norms reward endurance but discourage honest engagement. Over time, this focus on responsibility distorts identities, limits capacity, and undermines sustainability.

What often seems like individual burnout is, more accurately, architectural strain. Systems have relied on emotional self-sacrifice instead of shared stewardship. Leadership fatigue has been personalized rather than shared. Resilience has been praised without being supported by proper design.

Part I has not assigned blame. It has restored clarity.

When exhaustion is viewed as organizational feedback rather than personal weakness, leaders begin to identify where redistribution is necessary. When identity strain is acknowledged as a systemic risk, leaders develop language not only to protect themselves but also to collectively redesign expectations. When resilience is seen as shared responsibility rather than individual toughness, institutions become accountable for the environments they create. When emotional norms are clarified, culture becomes intentional rather than inherited.

This section has asked leaders to slow down enough to observe what has become normalized.

Not to dwell in discouragement — but to cultivate awareness strong enough to change design.

Because leadership renewal does not begin with action.

It begins with seeing.

Identifying where emotional labor is concentrated instead of shared. Recognizing where silence replaces partnership. Understanding where endurance is mistaken for effectiveness. Noticing where culture is shaped by avoidance instead of deliberate structure.

Part I establishes the foundation for what follows.

Once leaders recognize the emotional weight shaping their institutions, the focus shifts from diagnosis to redesign: How do we lead without taking on everything? How do we stay present without becoming overwhelmed? How do we handle complexity without centralizing responsibility?

Part II explores emotional integrity — not as a personality trait, but as a disciplined leadership approach maintained through shared containment. It looks at how leaders stay grounded while sharing relational effort, setting clear boundaries, and rebuilding trust without losing authority.

The work ahead is not about becoming softer leaders.

It's about developing steadier leaders — leaders who accept responsibility without taking it on all by themselves, who handle complexity without becoming cold, and who lead institutions forward through collaboration rather than sheer endurance.

Part I named the weight.

Part II begins the redesign — moving from concentrated strain toward shared responsibility.

# PART II

## LEADING WITH EMOTIONAL INTEGRITY IN EDUCATIONAL SYSTEMS

### Leading Faculty Without Micromanaging Autonomy

If Part I named the weight, Part II addresses the response.

In higher education, leadership rarely operates through direct control. Provosts, deans, department chairs, and program directors lead primarily through influence, credibility, and relational trust rather than hierarchy. Authority exists, but it is mediated through faculty governance, disciplinary norms, and institutional culture. Influence, not command, drives change.

This reality makes emotional anchoring essential. Postsecondary leaders must navigate tenure stress, departmental conflict, curriculum transformation, enrollment volatility, and early-career faculty development while balancing academic freedom with institutional responsibility. They are asked to protect autonomy while ensuring accountability, to safeguard scholarship while managing budget constraints, and to guide cultural shifts without appearing coercive.

Emotional steadiness becomes the mechanism through which influence remains credible.

The coaching and emotional leadership frameworks explored in this section translate directly into faculty environments where micromanagement erodes trust and disengagement fractures coherence. In these contexts, integrity is not optional. It is the foundation of sustainable influence.

## Emotional Integrity as Leadership Discipline

Once leaders understand the emotional realities shaping their schools and institutions, a deeper question emerges: How do you lead without taking everything in? How do you remain present without becoming depleted, respond without reacting, and show compassion without losing clarity?

Emotional integrity is not a personality trait. It is a disciplined stance. It is the ability to lead with steadiness, honesty, and relational awareness while maintaining internal coherence. It rejects both emotional overexposure and emotional suppression. Instead, it requires leaders to remain rooted in their values and role while navigating the emotional currents that move through educational systems every day.

Many institutions unintentionally train leaders to become emotional sponges—absorbing frustration, grief, anger, and anxiety to preserve outward calm. While this may maintain short-term stability, it is not sustainable. Leaders who absorb everything eventually lose clarity or capacity. Emotional integrity offers a different posture: anchoring rather than absorbing.

## From Containment to Anchoring

Emotionally intact leadership does not require leaders to carry others' emotional weight. It requires them to create conditions in which emotions can be acknowledged, processed, and directed constructively, without being displaced onto a single individual.

The shift is subtle but significant. It moves from holding emotions internally to intentionally holding space. It replaces performative calm with cultivated steadiness. It exchanges emotional self-sacrifice for emotionally responsible leadership. Leaders who anchor rather than absorb provide stability precisely because they do not internalize what is not theirs to carry. They model regulation rather than repression, clarity rather than detachment, and accountability rather than defensiveness.

This distinction matters profoundly in faculty leadership contexts where authority is relational and autonomy is valued. Anchored leadership protects both influence and integrity.

## Emotional Integrity Under Pressure

Emotional integrity is tested most sharply during policy shifts, staffing shortages, accreditation stress, campus unrest, and moments of collective frustration or grief. These are the conditions under which leaders are tempted to either overfunction emotionally or disengage entirely.

Leading with integrity under pressure requires more than technique. It requires a stance. It requires leaders to remain emotionally present without becoming emotionally entangled. It requires coaching without compounding stress, holding space without losing direction, repairing trust after missteps, and remaining steady when uncertainty intensifies.

Rather than offering scripts, this section emphasizes positioning—how leaders emotionally locate themselves in relation to others, the institution, and their own limits.

## Integrity as Structural Practice

While emotional integrity begins with personal awareness, it cannot remain purely individual. When integrity is isolated within a single office, emotional labor concentrates silently. When integrity is embedded systemically, responsibility becomes distributed and sustainable.

This means reinforcing integrity through clear role boundaries, thoughtful communication practices, relationally informed decision-making, and leadership norms that protect both people and purpose. Emotional intelligence is not a soft supplement to operational leadership. It is foundational to retention, morale, trust, and institutional resilience.

In both K–12 and higher education, integrity must move from individual virtue to structural design.

## A Bridge Between Reality and Renewal

Part I confronted what is breaking down. Part II explores how leaders hold what remains without losing themselves in the process.

This movement is not about becoming softer or more permissive. It is about becoming steadier and more sustainable. Leading with emotional integrity does not eliminate difficulty. It prevents difficulty from becoming corrosive.

In systems operating under sustained strain, that distinction defines longevity.

## Steadiness Within Shared Systems

Emotional integrity is often mistaken for composure under pressure. It is more demanding than that. It is the disciplined refusal to absorb every current moving through a system while remaining attentive to its impact. It is the capacity to anchor without rigidity, to respond without overreaction, and to lead without sacrificing internal clarity.

Yet integrity cannot remain solitary. When emotional labor is concentrated in a single office or role, even the most grounded leader becomes vulnerable to burnout. Sustainable steadiness requires shared containment. It requires structures that distribute responsibility for culture, conflict, and care rather than silently assigning those functions to one individual.

Emotional integrity begins within the leader, but its durability depends on how authority and expectation are architected across the system.

## Partnership Lens

Emotional integrity cannot depend on one leader's steadiness alone. Presence may stabilize culture temporarily, but partnership sustains it. When emotional containment is shared, leaders anchor without eroding. Authority matures when responsibility is distributed before pressure concentrates.

# CHAPTER 5

## THE PRINCIPAL AS EMOTIONAL ANCHOR, NOT EMOTIONAL SPONGE

### Global Leadership Spotlight

#### Country Focus: Finland
#### Principals as Emotional Anchors

Finland's education system is well-known for its focus on educator professionalism, institutional trust, and balanced leadership practices. Leadership training programs in Finland emphasize collaboration, shared responsibility, and relationship-based leadership alongside academic accountability. Instead of viewing principals as centralized authority figures, schools often adopt distributed leadership models that empower teachers, leadership teams, and support staff to be involved in decision-making.

Within this framework, school leaders are expected to provide emotional stability and strategic direction. Principals are trained to build trust, ensure psychological safety, and demonstrate calm, consistent presence during periods of change or pressure. This focus on relational leadership helps stabilize school culture by reducing fear-based management and enhancing professional autonomy.

Finland's approach highlights an important leadership principle: authority doesn't need to depend on control to be effective. When leadership is based on presence, clarity, and relational credibility, systems become more resilient. Emotional anchoring enables leaders to handle tension without passing it on and to guide teams through complexity without increasing stress.

**Leadership Reflection:**

In what ways does your leadership presence contribute to emotional stability—or emotional strain—within your organization?

Leadership does not fail because leaders care too much.

It fails when caring is confused with carrying everything alone.

In schools and educational institutions, leaders are often expected to absorb the emotional weight of the system—to take in frustration, fear, disappointment, anger, and uncertainty so that others can continue functioning. This expectation is rarely stated explicitly, yet it is reinforced through culture, role design, and professional norms. Leaders are praised for being calm under pressure, accessible to all, endlessly patient, and emotionally available at all times.

Over time, this unspoken expectation shapes how leaders understand their role. Many begin to equate effectiveness with absorption—believing that if they can hold everyone else's emotions, stability will follow.

It does not.

Leaders can't absorb everything and stay effective. What schools and institutions need are not emotional sponges but emotional anchors—leaders who offer stability without losing themselves, clarity without becoming detached, and compassion without breaking down.

This chapter introduces emotional anchoring as a foundational leadership stance: one that allows leaders to remain present and responsive without becoming depleted by what they are asked to hold.

## The Hidden Expectation to Absorb

In educational leadership, emotional absorption often masquerades as dedication. Leaders are expected to:

- Receive frustration without defensiveness
- Hold grief without slowing the system
- Contain anger without redirecting it
- Remain composed without acknowledging cost

When leaders do this well, systems continue to function. Meetings move forward. Conflict appears contained. Crises are managed. From the outside, leadership looks steady.

What is less visible is the internal cost of this role. Absorption requires leaders to take in emotion without expressing it outwardly. Over time, this causes emotional buildup—stress that settles rather than fades.

Many leaders fail to see this as a problem until clarity starts to fade. Decision-making becomes more difficult. Patience wears thin. Emotional connection requires more effort. The leader stays in position, but something vital begins to weaken.

This is not a failure of resilience or commitment. It is a consequence of a leadership model that mistakes emotional self-sacrifice for effectiveness.

## Emotional Anchoring: A Different Model

Emotional anchoring offers a fundamentally different approach.

An anchor does not absorb the force of the water; it provides stability within it. It holds steady without being pulled under. In leadership terms, anchoring means remaining grounded in one's role, values, and limits while allowing emotion to exist and move around—not through—the leader.

Anchoring is not emotional withdrawal; it is emotional presence with structure.

Emotionally anchored leaders:

- Acknowledge emotion without owning it
- Respond with clarity rather than reactivity
- Maintain boundaries without losing compassion
- Offer steadiness without suppressing humanity

This stance allows leaders to support others without becoming the sole container for the system's emotional weight.

## Grounded Presence

At the core of emotional anchoring is grounded presence.

Grounded presence is not the same as charisma or constant availability. It is the capacity to remain internally steady while engaging with emotionally charged situations. Leaders with grounded presence are not easily pulled into urgency, panic, or overidentification. They listen carefully, respond deliberately, and resist the pressure to resolve everything immediately.

In practice, grounded presence looks like:

- Pausing before responding to emotionally charged feedback
- Asking clarifying questions rather than reacting defensively
- Naming uncertainty honestly without amplifying anxiety
- Holding space for emotion without rushing to fix it

This presence is especially vital during times of collective stress—such as policy changes, staffing shifts, crises, or periods of mourning. When leaders stay grounded, they demonstrate regulation for the entire system.

Importantly, grounded presence does not demand emotional suppression. It calls for self-connection—an awareness of one's own emotional state and the ability to remain anchored within it.

## Clear Boundaries

Emotional anchoring is impossible without boundaries.

Boundaries clarify what leaders are responsible for and what they are not. They protect leaders from overfunctioning emotionally while ensuring they remain accountable and responsive.

Clear emotional boundaries allow leaders to:

- Support without rescuing
- Listen without absorbing
- Care without overidentifying
- Lead without becoming emotionally overextended

In educational environments, boundary confusion frequently happens because of a desire to help. Leaders might feel the need to always be available, take on extra emotional work, or protect others from feeling uncomfortable. Although well-meaning, this approach can ultimately hurt long-term sustainability.

Boundaries are not barriers. They are structures that make care sustainable.

When leaders clearly define boundaries—such as availability, decision-making authority, and emotional responsibilities—they reduce confusion and prevent emotional exhaustion. Staff understand what support looks like, and leaders can stay present over time.

## Leadership Moment: Holding the Line Without Hardening

The parent meeting escalated quickly. Frustration turned into accusation. Voices rose. Emotion filled the room.

The administrator felt the familiar surge—the instinct to absorb the tension, to defend decisions, to fix the situation immediately. Instead, they grounded their posture, slowed their breathing, and spoke calmly.

"I hear how much this situation matters to you," they said. "We will address it. But we will do so with respect."

The conflict did not disappear. The problem was not instantly solved. But something important shifted. The emotional temperature dropped. The conversation stabilized. The room became safer.

This is emotional anchoring. It is not emotional distance. It is leadership presence that fosters psychological safety without compromising boundaries. It is the ability to stay steady without becoming rigid, compassionate without becoming overwhelmed.

## Emotional Steadiness Without Self-Erasure

One of the most persistent myths in leadership is that emotional steadiness requires emotional disappearance.

In reality, emotional steadiness isn't about becoming less human. It's about becoming more integrated—by aligning emotional awareness with your professional role.

Emotionally anchored leaders do not deny their feelings. They recognize, regulate, and prevent these feelings from taking over their leadership. This helps leaders stay authentic without becoming the center of attention during moments that require collective focus.

Self-erasure, by contrast, occurs when leaders regularly suppress their emotions to appear unshakable. Over time, this can cause disconnection, resentment, or burnout.

Emotional integrity requires leaders to stay whole—leading from a place where their values, emotions, and responsibilities are aligned rather than fragmented.

## Why Anchoring Matters Now

In systems under prolonged stress, leadership presence becomes a stabilizing influence. When leaders take on everything, the system might seem calm for a while—but the leader eventually breaks down. When leaders provide stability, the system learns to self-regulate more effectively.

Anchoring shifts culture in subtle but powerful ways:

- Emotion becomes shared rather than concentrated

- Accountability replaces emotional dumping
- Trust grows through consistency rather than sacrifice
- Sustainability becomes possible without disengagement

This chapter does not ask leaders to care less.

It asks them to care more responsibly.

Leading as an emotional anchor protects not only the leader but also the institution itself. It demonstrates a form of leadership capable of managing complexity without breaking down.

The upcoming chapters will examine how emotional anchoring appears in coaching, communication, trust repair, and change leadership. However, anchoring starts here—with the understanding that stability isn't achieved through absorption.

It comes from grounded presence, clear boundaries, and emotional steadiness without self-erasure.

That is the work of emotionally intact leadership.

# INSIDE THE CLASSROOM

## The Weight Leaders Don't Show

The assistant principal stood in the hallway during dismissal, responding to a frustrated parent on the phone while monitoring student traffic and answering a teacher's quick question about coverage. Their voice remained calm. Their posture was steady. No one could see the tension tightening across their shoulders.

Later that evening, they replayed the conversation in their mind. They wondered if they had been too firm. Too soft. Too careful. The emotional calculus of leadership rarely ends when the building empties.

What most people saw was composure. What they did not see was the build-up of moments like these — small emotional negotiations layered throughout the day. Each one demands presence, restraint, and steady control.

Leadership often rewards outward calm without recognizing the internal toll of sustaining it. Emotional anchoring is not easy;

it demands energy, discipline, and deliberate recovery. Without that recovery time, even the most steady leaders start to shoulder more than they should.

---

# LEADERSHIP NEXT STEPS —
## Principals as Emotional Anchors

 **Awareness Shift: Distinguish Anchoring From Absorbing**

Many school leaders confuse emotional availability with emotional absorption. Over time, this blurs boundaries and leads to burnout. Emotional anchoring requires leaders to stay present without taking on the emotional weight of the system.

Start noticing when you're taking responsibility for stabilizing emotions rather than processes. Pay attention to moments when you feel the urge to "hold everything together" emotionally. These moments show where anchoring can replace absorption.

**Ask yourself:**

Where am I taking on emotional stress that should be handled through leadership rather than personal endurance?

 **Leadership Behavior Adjustment: Practice Grounded Presence**

Anchoring starts with grounded presence. Leaders who stay emotionally steady during tension foster psychological safety without losing clarity or authority. This doesn't mean emotional distance. Instead, it requires self-regulation, deliberate pacing, and awareness of relationships.

Leaders model grounded presence when they:

- Pause before responding to emotionally charged situations
- Speak with calm clarity rather than urgency
- Maintain composure without suppressing humanity
- Listen without rushing to fix or rescue

When leaders regulate themselves, they help the entire system regulate more effectively.

 **Structural or Cultural Reinforcement: Build Boundary-Supported Leadership Norms**

Emotional anchoring becomes sustainable only when supported by a clear structure. Without well-defined leadership norms and role boundaries, principals are often expected to be constantly available, emotionally responsive, and personally responsible for maintaining the system.

Identify one structural adjustment that protects emotional boundaries, such as:

- Clarifying availability expectations for leadership roles
- Redesigning crisis response processes to reduce emotional concentration
- Establishing shared leadership responsibility for relational work
- Creating protected time for leadership reflection and recovery

When boundaries are structurally supported, emotional steadiness becomes sustainable rather than performative.

> ## Leadership Anchor:
> ## Lead With Presence Without
> ## Self-Erasure
>
> Emotional anchoring is not emotional withdrawal. It is leadership presence rooted in clarity, boundaries, and steadiness. Principals do not need to disappear emotionally to lead effectively; they need to stay connected without being overwhelmed by the system's emotional load. Sustainable leadership occurs when presence is strong enough to stabilize others while protecting the leader's identity and capacity.

## Partnership as Leadership Architecture

Anchoring does not require absorption. When a single office becomes the emotional container for an entire system, burnout speeds up behind the façade of professionalism. Partnership shares containment across leadership layers, so presence remains consistent without self-erasure. Authority matures when responsibility is distributed before pressure builds.

# CHAPTER 6

## COACHING WITHOUT CRUSHING:
## HOW TO LEAD TEACHERS UNDER PRESSURE

**Country Focus: Singapore**
**Coaching Under Pressure**

Singapore's education system is globally recognized for its strong academic results and clear pathways for leadership development. The Ministry of Education has invested heavily in leadership pipelines focused on ongoing professional learning, mentorship, and instructional coaching. School leaders are nurtured through formal training programs, leadership rotations, and continuous professional development designed to prepare them for complex organizational and instructional challenges.

High performance expectations remain central to the system, but they are supported by institutional structures that focus on building leadership capacity. Instead of relying only on hierarchical evaluation, many schools prioritize coaching conversations, reflective practices, and collaborative professional learning communities. This approach enables leaders to uphold high standards while fostering educator growth.

Singapore's example demonstrates a key leadership lesson: pressure doesn't have to be harsh or emotional. Achieving high performance can go hand in hand with relational leadership when development is viewed as an investment, not just compliance. Coaching cultures safeguard both standards and people by encouraging trust, clarity, and psychological safety.

**Leadership Reflection:**

How are leaders in your organization equipped to develop others in ways that strengthen performance without eroding morale or professional confidence?

In high-stress environments, feedback is rarely neutral.

What leaders see as support is often felt as a threat. What is given as guidance can come across as judgment. And what is presented as growth can, under pressure, increase exhaustion rather than develop capacity.

Leaders are not lacking in skill or care; instead, coaching occurs within emotional contexts shaped by workload, trust, fear, history, and identity. Ignoring these contexts can turn well-meaning feedback into harm.

This chapter examines a core tension in educational leadership: how to foster professional growth without increasing stress. It redefines coaching not as a technique, but as a relational act that must be emotionally sequenced, not just strategically planned.

## When Feedback Becomes a Stress Multiplier

Coaching is often seen as naturally supportive. However, many educators say feedback conversations are among the most emotionally draining moments of their work—not because they resist growth, but because feedback comes on top of exhaustion.

In systems under strain, feedback can become a stress multiplier. Educators are already navigating:

- Increased workload and reduced planning time
- Emotional labor related to student needs
- Shifting expectations and initiative overload
- Uncertainty about evaluation, security, or role clarity

When feedback enters this landscape without attention to emotional load, it risks reinforcing a sense of inadequacy rather than fostering development.

Leaders might notice that teachers seem defensive, withdrawn, or overwhelmed during coaching conversations. Too often, this is seen as resistance. In truth, it is often a stress response—a sign that the nervous system is already working at capacity.

In such moments, more feedback does not produce better outcomes. It produces shutdown, compliance, or quiet disengagement.

## Trauma-Aware Coaching: A Necessary Lens

Trauma-aware coaching doesn't require leaders to become therapists, nor does it assume that every educator is experiencing trauma in a clinical way. Instead, it recognizes a core truth: chronic stress changes how people process information.

Under sustained pressure, educators may:

- Interpret feedback as a threat rather than support.
- Struggle to process nuance or complexity
- Fixate on perceived failure rather than opportunity
- Experience feedback as confirmation of inadequacy

Trauma-aware coaching understands that emotional state affects cognitive ability. It emphasizes psychological safety not just as a source of comfort, but as essential for learning.

Key principles of trauma-aware coaching include:

- Assuming stress before assuming resistance
- Slowing down rather than intensifying pressure
- Separating performance from identity
- Offering clarity without urgency

This approach does not reduce standards. It establishes the conditions necessary to achieve the standards.

## Timing Matters More Than Content

One of the most overlooked aspects of effective coaching is timing.

Leaders often focus on *what* to say while underestimating *when* to say it. In high-stress environments, poorly timed feedback—no matter how accurate—can feel punitive.

Timing is not about avoidance. It is about discernment.

Effective leaders learn to ask:

- Is this educator emotionally resourced enough to hear this now?
- Is this moment about support or accountability?
- Will feedback here build capacity—or trigger defensiveness?

There are times when immediate feedback is essential for safety, compliance, or student well-being. However, many coaching conversations can—and should—be postponed until the educator has enough bandwidth to engage constructively.

Delaying feedback isn't the same as ignoring issues. It's a leadership decision that prioritizes impact over immediacy.

## Tone as a Leadership Tool

Tone carries meaning before content ever does.

In high-stress environments, educators become highly sensitive to tone—not because they are overly reactive, but because tone indicates safety, threat, respect, or dismissal. Leaders might think their tone is neutral, but educators often perceive it as sharp, hurried, or judgmental.

Tone doesn't mean softness; it signifies alignment between message and intention.

Supportive tone in coaching includes:

- Curiosity rather than assumption
- Specificity rather than generalization
- Invitation rather than interrogation
- Calm rather than urgency

Leaders who master tone understand that how feedback is delivered often determines whether it is heard at all. A regulated tone models emotional steadiness and communicates that growth is a shared goal, not a test of worth.

## Supporting Growth Without Adding Weight

One of the toughest leadership challenges is helping improve systems that are already overwhelmed. When expectations increase without easing other pressures, growth turns into an additional burden.

Effective coaching under pressure requires leaders to focus on load, not just performance.

This means asking:

- What can reasonably be asked right now?
- What support must accompany this expectation?
- What can be removed, paused, or deprioritized to make space for growth?

Growth that ignores capacity is unsustainable. It leads to surface compliance rather than deep development.

Leaders can support growth without compounding stress by:

- Narrowing focus rather than expanding it
- Offering fewer, clearer priorities
- Acknowledging effort alongside outcome
- Distinguishing between developmental feedback and evaluative judgment

When educators feel that leaders understand the weight they are carrying, feedback becomes collaborative rather than corrective.

## Coaching as Relationship, Not Intervention

Coaching is often treated as an event—a scheduled meeting, a documented observation, a formal conversation. In reality, its effectiveness is shaped long before the conversation begins.

Educators are more receptive to feedback when they experience leaders as:

- Consistent rather than performative
- Predictable rather than reactive
- Fair rather than punitive
- Human rather than distant

This is why emotionally anchored leadership matters. Leaders who have established trust through presence and clear boundaries create relational conditions in which feedback can land without crushing.

Coaching without crushing involves leaders viewing growth as a long-term relationship, not just a corrective exchange.

## The Leader's Role in Emotional Regulation

Coaching conversations often evoke emotion—not just in educators, but also in leaders. Frustration, urgency, disappointment, or anxiety can subtly influence how feedback is given.

Emotionally balanced leaders attend to their own internal state before entering coaching spaces. They understand that unregulated leadership emotion is contagious.

Leaders who rush into feedback while dysregulated may:

- Overemphasize deficits
- Escalate tone unintentionally
- Seek relief rather than growth
- Confuse clarity with control

Regulated leaders, by contrast, can manage complexity. They can recognize concerns without exaggerating them, focus on performance without making it personal, and stay steady even when conversations become uncomfortable.

This self-regulation is not incidental. It is a core leadership skill.

## Redefining Effective Coaching

Coaching without crushing requires a redefinition of effectiveness.

Effective coaching does not lead to immediate compliance.

It builds lasting capacity.

It does not leave educators feeling smaller.

It leaves them feeling clearer.

It does not rely on pressure.

It relies on trust, timing, and emotional integrity.

In systems under strain, leaders will always face pressure to fix, correct, and accelerate. This chapter offers a different invitation: to coach in ways that protect the nervous system, honor professional dignity, and build long-term resilience without relying on personal sacrifice.

The next chapters will continue this exploration—examining how leaders hold space for frustration and grief, repair trust after missteps, and lead change without eroding the people tasked with carrying it.

But the foundation is here.

Coaching can either strengthen or crush.

The key is not intent but emotional awareness, timing, and integrity.

And in the schools and institutions of today, that difference matters more than ever.

# INSIDE THE CLASSROOM

## After the Feedback Conversation

The instructional coach closed the classroom door gently behind them. The feedback conversation had gone well on the surface. The teacher nodded, took notes, and thanked them for the support.

But as the coach walked back to their office, they felt uneasy. Something about the interaction stayed with them. The teacher's posture had been stiff. Their smile was polite but faint. The words had been received, but the emotional impact was unclear.

Later that week, the teacher avoided eye contact during a staff meeting. Participation dropped. Engagement shifted.

Feedback does not only carry information. It carries emotional meaning. Even well-intended coaching can leave people feeling exposed, judged, or quietly discouraged if timing and tone are misaligned.

Leadership under pressure requires more than delivering content. It requires awareness of how growth conversations shape safety, trust, and identity in the room.

## LEADERSHIP NEXT STEPS — Coaching Under Pressure

 **Awareness Shift: Separate Support From Control**

Under pressure, coaching often shifts into correction, monitoring, or performance management. While accountability is necessary, leadership effectiveness depends on distinguishing between support that strengthens professional growth and control that suppresses autonomy.

Begin noticing when feedback conversations are driven by urgency, compliance demands, or institutional anxiety rather than developmental intent. These moments reveal where coaching may unintentionally become coercive rather than collaborative.

**Ask yourself:**

Where has coaching shifted from developmental partnership to performance enforcement?

 **Leadership Behavior Adjustment: Practice Pressure-Aware Coaching**

Coaching under pressure requires emotional regulation, timing awareness, and relational skill. Leaders must learn to address performance concerns without escalating stress or eroding trust.

Pressure-aware coaching includes behaviors such as:

- Choosing timing that allows for reflection rather than emotional reactivity
- Framing feedback around growth rather than deficiency
- Listening for emotional context, not just instructional outcomes
- Balancing clarity with empathy

When leaders coach with awareness of pressure, feedback becomes stabilizing rather than destabilizing.

 **Structural or Cultural Reinforcement: Build Coaching Into Leadership Systems**

Coaching cannot remain an informal or optional leadership behavior. When it lacks support from structure, it becomes inconsistent and relies on individual leadership styles. A sustainable coaching culture needs institutional reinforcement.

Identify one structural adjustment that strengthens coaching practice, such as:

- Creating protected time for instructional coaching conversations
- Standardizing feedback frameworks that emphasize development
- Training leadership teams in coaching communication skills
- Aligning evaluation systems with growth-oriented feedback

When coaching is structurally supported, leaders are less likely to default to command-and-control responses under stress.

---

## Leadership Anchor:
## Influence Without Intimidation

Coaching under pressure tests leadership maturity. The easiest response is to tighten control. The strongest response is to maintain influence without intimidation. Effective leaders create clarity without fear, accountability without humiliation, and growth without emotional damage. When coaching is rooted in trust and emotional integrity, it strengthens professional capacity rather than weakening morale.

## Partnership as Leadership Architecture 

Feedback under pressure needs accuracy rather than prediction. Fixing without understanding relationships breaks trust and limits growth. Partnership views development as joint improvement, not enforced rules. Accountability is stronger when clarity and compassion work together.

# CHAPTER 7

## HOLDING SPACE FOR FRUSTRATION, GRIEF, AND CHANGE FATIGUE

### Global Leadership Spotlight

**Country Focus: New Zealand
Holding Space for Emotional Processing**

New Zealand's education system has increasingly focused on trauma-informed and culturally responsive leadership practices, especially in response to national crises and large-scale disruptions. After events that significantly affected communities, education leaders were encouraged to prioritize emotional safety, collective healing, and building trust, alongside maintaining academic progress. Policies and professional development programs have helped school leaders understand the emotional effects of crises on students, staff, and families.

This shift highlights an essential leadership principle: emotional processing is integral to institutional recovery—it is at its core. When leaders recognize grief, fear, and uncertainty instead of dismissing them, they foster environments where people feel acknowledged and supported. Emotional honesty helps teams stabilize more effectively by preventing unresolved stress from later manifesting as conflict, disengagement, or burnout.

New Zealand's approach emphasizes that emotional expression is not a weakness. It serves as valuable leadership data, offering insight into organizational health, team capacity, and community needs. Leaders who can hold space for emotion without becoming overwhelmed build trust and foster long-term resilience.

**Leadership Reflection:**

Where might greater emotional honesty improve trust, communication, and stability within your organization?

In many educational settings, emotional expression is regarded as a problem to control rather than information to grasp. Frustration is perceived as resistance. Grief is seen as a distraction. Fatigue is understood as disengagement. Leaders, under pressure to maintain momentum, often learn—either consciously or unconsciously—to move conversations past emotion as quickly as possible.

This approach is understandable. Schools and institutions must operate. Learning must go on. Decisions must be made. But when emotional expression is consistently ignored, it doesn't go away. It becomes ingrained—shaping behavior, relationships, and culture in ways that are far more disruptive than emotions acknowledged and intentionally addressed.

This chapter redefines emotional expression not as disruption but as valuable data. Frustration, grief, and fatigue give leaders important insights into what systems are requesting from people, where trust has been strained, and where capacity has been overextended. When leaders learn to interpret this data rather than suppress it, they unlock information that policy alone cannot provide.

## Frustration as Signal, Not Threat

Frustration often appears at the edges of change. It shows up when expectations don't match reality, when communication isn't clear, or when people are asked to do more than they can handle. In schools and colleges, frustration is often seen as defiance or negativity, especially when it challenges leadership decisions.

Yet frustration is rarely about opposition alone. More often, it is about strain.

When leaders dismiss frustration, they miss a chance to understand where systems clash with human limits. When they approach it thoughtfully, frustration becomes a diagnostic tool—highlighting pressure points that, if ignored, will eventually weaken implementation and morale.

Holding space for frustration doesn't mean agreeing with every concern or stopping progress forever. It means letting frustration be expressed without punishment, recognizing it without defensiveness, and responding with curiosity instead of control. Leaders who do this consistently lessen the chance that frustration will turn into disengagement or quiet resistance.

## Naming Grief Without Losing Forward Motion

Grief in educational settings is often unseen because there isn't a single, clear event marking it. Instead, it builds quietly through losses that are hard to measure: autonomy, time, trust, and professional identity as roles evolve.

Leaders also carry grief—often without words to express it. They mourn the profession they chose, the relationships changed by policy decisions, and the sense of possibility that once felt more within reach.

Because grief slows down emotional systems, leaders might feel pressured to push through it quickly. However, unacknowledged grief doesn't just go away with time. Instead, it reemerges as cynicism, detachment, or resistance to change—not because people are unwilling to move forward, but because they haven't been given the opportunity to process what they've lost.

Naming grief is not an act of stagnation. It is an act of clarification.

When leaders acknowledge loss openly—without dramatization or apology—they validate emotional experience without losing sight of their goals. Grief can be identified without dominating every conversation. It can be respected without stopping progress. In fact, momentum often returns more effectively when people feel their experience has been recognized rather than ignored.

## Change Fatigue as Cumulative Load

Change fatigue isn't about being unable to adapt. Educators are constantly adapting. It's about the toll of volume without time to recover.

In environments where initiatives arrive faster than they can be integrated, people begin to experience change not as growth, but as erosion. Even positive reforms can become exhausting when layered without removal, when the rationale is unclear, or when outcomes remain uncertain.

Leaders might see hesitation about new initiatives as a lack of commitment. More often, it shows they are overwhelmed.

Holding space for change fatigue requires leaders to slow the emotional pace of change, even when operational timelines cannot be shifted. This may involve recognizing the cumulative nature of recent demands, clarifying priorities, and clearly stating what will not be added—or what will be paused—to make room for what matters most.

When leaders recognize fatigue as a cumulative load rather than an attitude, they are better positioned to maintain trust as they move forward.

## Leadership Moment: The Department Chair Check-In

Over several weeks, the department chair observed a change in meetings. More tension. Shorter responses. Quiet disengagement. Instead of pushing harder for productivity, they started the next meeting differently.

"Before we talk strategy," they said, "what is one pressure you're carrying this week?"

The responses came slowly at first. Then more openly. Grief. Caregiving responsibilities. Emotional exhaustion. Professional uncertainty.

Nothing was resolved at that moment. No policies were changed. No workloads disappeared. Yet, something meaningful occurred. Trust grew. Engagement softened. People felt acknowledged.

Leadership does not always solve problems. Sometimes it stabilizes people long enough for them to stay connected to the work.

## Facilitating Difficult Conversations with Structure

Difficult conversations are unavoidable in education. The question is not whether they will occur, but how they are held.

Leaders who avoid difficult conversations often do so out of concern for morale or fear of escalation. Leaders who rush through them often do so to regain control. Neither approach creates psychological safety.

Effective facilitation requires a clear structure. Leaders must define the purpose of the conversation, clarify what is open for discussion, and specify decisions that have already been made. Ambiguity in situations with high emotions increases anxiety instead of easing it.

At the same time, a structure lacking emotional awareness can feel stiff. Leaders must focus not only on content but also on pacing, tone, and acknowledgment. Difficult conversations go more smoothly when leaders can identify tension without making it worse and manage disagreement without taking it personally.

When leaders facilitate with both clarity and presence, difficult conversations become spaces for alignment rather than fracture.

## Honesty Without Professional Erosion

One of the most persistent fears in educational leadership is that allowing honesty will erode professionalism. Leaders worry that open emotional expression will lead to venting, loss of control, or diminished authority.

This fear often leads to emotional containment strategies that prioritize composure over authenticity. Yet professionalism does not require emotional absence. It requires emotional regulation.

Allowing honesty doesn't mean opening every space to unfiltered expression. It means creating specific moments where concerns can be raised, named, and addressed within clear boundaries. It means responding to honesty with respect rather than punishment. And it means showing how emotion and professionalism can coexist.

Leaders set the emotional tone. When they respond to honesty with steadiness rather than defensiveness, they teach the system how to handle truth without chaos.

## Emotional Expression as Leadership Intelligence

Emotion is already shaping schools and institutions—whether leaders engage it or not. The difference lies in whether emotion is treated as interference or information.

Leaders who dismiss emotional expression miss out on vital insight. Leaders who indulge it without guidance lose their way. Leaders who interpret it gain clarity.

Holding space isn't about always being emotionally available. It's about knowing when and how to allow expression, listening for meaning beneath words, and translating emotional signals into thoughtful leadership actions.

This chapter doesn't expect leaders to act as counselors. Instead, it asks them to become emotionally intelligent decision-makers—able to handle frustration, grief, and fatigue without losing focus.

In systems under sustained pressure, emotional truth is not the enemy of progress.

Unacknowledged emotion is.

The chapters that follow will continue to explore how emotionally intact leaders repair trust, navigate missteps, and lead change without fracturing themselves or their institutions.

But that work relies on this fundamental shift: recognizing that what people feel is not noise to be silenced, but information to be interpreted—carefully, responsibly, and with integrity.

## INSIDE THE CLASSROOM

### When the Room Needed Space

The department meeting was scheduled to review the new curriculum changes. Instead, it turned into something else entirely.

One teacher spoke about exhaustion. Another admitted feeling overwhelmed. Someone quietly shared that they were considering leaving at the end of the year.

The administrator felt the familiar tension between moving the agenda forward and honoring the emotional moment unfolding. They chose to pause the presentation and let the conversation breathe.

No decisions were finalized that day. No timelines were approved. But something important happened. People stayed. They listened. They felt less alone.

Sometimes leadership is not about accelerating progress. Sometimes it is about creating enough emotional space for people to remain connected to the work.

# LEADERSHIP NEXT STEPS —
## Holding Space for Emotional Processing

 **Awareness Shift: Normalize Emotional Processing as Leadership Work**

Frustration, grief, and change fatigue are not distractions from leadership — they are part of the leadership landscape. When these emotions are ignored or minimized, they do not disappear. They resurface as disengagement, resistance, or quiet burnout.

Begin recognizing emotional processing as legitimate leadership work rather than an optional relational add-on. Notice where emotions are routinely bypassed in favor of productivity, efficiency, or policy compliance. These patterns reveal where leaders may be unintentionally reinforcing emotional suppression.

**Ask yourself:**

Where are emotional realities being rushed past rather than intentionally addressed?

 **Leadership Behavior Adjustment: Practice Containment Without Suppression**

Holding space does not mean absorbing emotion or abandoning professional boundaries. It means creating conditions where people can express emotional reality without destabilizing the system. Leaders must learn to remain present during emotional intensity without rushing to fix, dismiss, or redirect prematurely.

Leaders practice healthy containment when they:

- Listen without immediately offering solutions
- Validate emotional experience without amplifying conflict
- Maintain calm presence during difficult conversations
- Slow conversations when emotional escalation occurs

When leaders contain their emotions without suppressing them, trust deepens, and relational repair becomes possible.

###  Structural or Cultural Reinforcement: Create Institutional Processing Pathways

Emotional processing cannot rely solely on individual leaders' relational skills. Institutions must create formal spaces and practices that allow emotional realities to be addressed collectively and constructively.

Identify one structural practice that supports emotional processing, such as:

- Integrating reflection time into staff meetings
- Establishing peer support or facilitated dialogue spaces
- Creating structured debrief processes after high-stress events
- Training leaders in trauma-informed communication

When emotional processing is supported structurally, leaders are no longer required to carry relational weight alone.

---

## " Leadership Anchor: Hold Emotion Without Letting It Define the System

Effective leaders do not eliminate emotional expression. They prevent it from overwhelming the organization. Holding space means acknowledging emotional reality while maintaining forward movement, stability, and shared purpose. When leaders treat emotional processing as part of institutional health rather than as a source of disruption, they strengthen trust, resilience, and the collective capacity for change.

## Partnership as Leadership Architecture

Emotion is data, not disruption. When leaders' silence becomes strained, it reemerges as resistance, withdrawal, or disengagement. Partnership validates expression without sacrificing direction. Stability grows when systems learn to manage complexity collectively rather than forcing individuals to handle it alone.

# CHAPTER 8

## REPAIRING TRUST AFTER LEADERSHIP MISSTEPS AND POLICY SHIFTS

**Global Leadership Spotlight**

**Country Focus: Canada**
**Repairing Trust After Institutional Harm**

Across Canada, education systems continue long-term reconciliation efforts with Indigenous communities, addressing the legacy of residential schools and systemic inequities within public institutions. National frameworks, including the Truth and Reconciliation Commission's Calls to Action, emphasize educational leaders' responsibility to confront historical harm through curriculum reform, community partnerships, and institutional accountability.

These efforts show that rebuilding trust isn't a one-time act or symbolic gesture. It requires ongoing relationship work, honest acknowledgment of harm, and meaningful structural change. School leaders are increasingly expected to have tough conversations, listen to affected communities, and adapt institutional practices to reflect respect, inclusion, and shared responsibility.

Canada's experience illustrates a broader leadership principle: integrity isn't just measured by policies enacted or decisions made under favorable conditions. It's assessed by how leaders respond when trust has been broken. Repair-focused leadership requires humility, presence, and the willingness to stay engaged even when progress is slow or uncomfortable. When leaders prioritize relational repair alongside institutional accountability, they enhance both moral credibility and organizational stability.

**Leadership Reflection:**

When trust has been damaged in your organization, how have leaders responded—and what structures could better support long-term repair rather than short-term resolution?

Trust is not restored through explanation.

It is restored through presence and repair.

In educational systems, trust is often taken for granted as being durable, something that can survive missteps, setbacks, and imposed changes as long as leaders communicate effectively. When trust breaks down, the natural reaction is to explain: to justify decisions, clarify intentions, outline constraints, and restate purpose. Although explanation plays a role, it is rarely enough.

Trust is relational, not transactional. When it is strained or broken, people are not asking for more information; they are asking whether leadership is willing to acknowledge impact, stay present through discomfort, and engage in repair without defensiveness.

This chapter explores what it means to rebuild trust after leadership missteps and policy shifts—particularly in environments already fatigued and emotionally strained.

## How Trust Is Quietly Lost

Trust in schools and institutions is rarely lost in a single moment. More often, it erodes incrementally through a series of experiences that signal misalignment between words and actions.

Trust weakens when leaders:

- Announce decisions without acknowledging impact
- Solicit input without demonstrating how it mattered
- Change direction without naming the cost of change
- Prioritize optics over relationship

These moments may seem small in isolation. Over time, they accumulate into a pattern. Educators begin to anticipate disappointment. They lower expectations for transparency. They disengage emotionally while continuing to comply professionally.

Importantly, trust erosion is not always caused by poor intent. Leaders often operate within constraints—such as policy mandates, funding limitations, and political pressure—that restrict their choices. The harm arises not just from the decision itself, but from how it is perceived relationally.

When leaders underestimate the emotional effect of decisions, trust slowly breaks down.

## Accountability Without Collapse

Leadership accountability is often mistaken for self-criticism or a public apology. In reality, accountability is neither performative nor self-punishing. It is the willingness to acknowledge impact without retreating into justification or defensiveness.

Accountability feels more like acknowledgment than explanation. It focuses on experience rather than intent. It identifies misalignment without exaggeration.

In practice, accountable leadership requires a straightforward but challenging shift: from asking why we did this to understanding how it impacted you.

This does not mean leaders assume responsibility for everything that goes wrong. It means they take responsibility for their role in shaping circumstances, communication, and response. Accountability does not weaken authority. When practiced consistently, it enhances credibility.

Leaders who exemplify accountability show that trust is more important than appearance. They demonstrate that leadership isn't about being perfect, but about being dependable in relationships.

## Repair Requires Staying Power

Repair is not a moment. It is a process.

One of the most common mistakes leaders make after a misstep is moving on too quickly. Once a concern has been addressed—or an apology offered —leaders may feel pressure to shift focus to future goals. While progress is important, rushing the process can increase distrust.

Repair involves remaining present after the initial conversation. It requires leaders to accept discomfort without rushing to fix things. It also demands consistency—showing up again, listening again, and following through over time.

In schools and universities, this may involve revisiting decisions, adjusting implementation, or acknowledging ongoing frustration without reopening every debate. Repair does not mean reversing every choice. It means demonstrating that relationships have not been sacrificed for efficiency.

Trust is rebuilt when people see that leaders remain engaged even after the spotlight fades.

## Policy Shifts and Relational Fallout

Policy changes—particularly those imposed from outside the institution—present unique challenges for trust. Leaders are often tasked with implementing decisions they did not make, within timelines they did not control. In these moments, leaders can become symbolic stand-ins for the system itself.

Educators may project anger, disappointment, or grief onto leadership—not because leaders caused the change, but because they are the most immediate relational presence.

Leaders who respond defensively in these moments often escalate distrust. Leaders who distance themselves emotionally may preserve composure but lose connection. Neither approach fosters repair.

Emotionally resilient leaders honestly acknowledge the stress caused by policy changes. They recognize their limits without shirking responsibility. They do not downplay the impact, even when choices are limited.

This stance demands humility and clarity. It also requires leaders to avoid the temptation to hide behind language like "we have no choice" to disengage relationally. Even when options are limited, being present is still possible.

## Rebuilding Credibility Without Defensiveness

Defensiveness is one of the greatest obstacles to trust repair.

When leaders feel misunderstood, criticized, or unfairly blamed, defensiveness can quickly emerge. It might show up as over-explaining, dismissing concerns, or shifting focus back to rationale and intent. Although understandable, defensiveness indicates emotional distance rather than care.

Credibility is rebuilt when leaders demonstrate that they can hear difficult feedback without needing to protect themselves from it. This does not mean accepting all criticism as valid. It means listening long enough to understand why trust has been strained.

Leaders who rebuild credibility effectively do so through consistency rather than persuasion. They align words with actions. They communicate predictably. They follow through on commitments— even small ones.

Over time, credibility returns not because leaders convinced others, but because they proved themselves reliable again.

## Trust as a Living System

Trust is not a static asset that can be restored and set aside. It is a living system that requires ongoing attention—particularly in environments marked by change and pressure.

Emotionally intelligent leadership views trust as something to be maintained through consistent effort, not only repaired after a crisis. It understands that trust develops when leaders are visible, responsive, and willing to engage relationally, even amid uncertainty.

This chapter clarifies that leaders do not need to be constantly available or emotionally vulnerable. Instead, it emphasizes that leaders should be relationally present—willing to stay engaged in conversations, acknowledge their impact, and demonstrate integrity when mistakes happen.

In systems under strain, trust will inevitably be tested. The question is not whether leaders will face moments of fracture, but whether they will respond with avoidance or repair.

Trust is not restored through explanation.

It is restored through presence, accountability, and sustained follow-through.

The following chapters will expand on this work by examining how emotionally healthy leadership encourages cultural adaptability, identity flexibility, and shared caring. However, this effort relies on this base.

Because without trust, no system—no matter how well designed—can truly hold the people within it.

# INSIDE THE CLASSROOM

## The Long Road Back to Trust

After a controversial policy shift, staff morale dipped sharply. Meetings became quiet. Emails grew shorter. Informal conversations disappeared.

The principal noticed the change but resisted the urge to explain the decision again. Instead, they started appearing differently, visiting classrooms more frequently, listening without defensiveness, and openly acknowledging the strain.

Rebuilding trust doesn't happen after just one meeting or apology. It takes time, consistency, presence, and a willingness to stay available even when it's uncomfortable.

Trust is rarely restored through statements. It is rebuilt through behavior repeated over time.

Leadership repair requires patience. It requires humility. And it requires the courage to remain visible when retreat would feel easier.

---

## LEADERSHIP NEXT STEPS — Repairing Trust After Institutional Harm

 **Awareness Shift: Recognize Trust Loss as a Leadership Responsibility**

Trust does not erode only because of individual mistakes. It is often damaged by policy shifts, communication breakdowns, and institutional decisions that disrupt stability or ignore lived experience. When trust fractures, leaders may be tempted to move forward quickly without addressing the relational impact. Sustainable leadership requires acknowledging trust loss as a leadership responsibility rather than a public relations issue.

Begin noticing where people disengage, withdraw, or become skeptical. These responses signal unresolved relational harm that cannot be repaired through messaging alone.

**Ask yourself:**

Where has institutional change created relational damage that remains unaddressed?

 **Leadership Behavior Adjustment: Practice Transparent and Accountable Communication**

Repair begins with honesty. Leaders must learn to communicate clearly about missteps, uncertainty, and impact without defensiveness or image management. Transparent communication does not require oversharing. It requires acknowledging reality, naming harm where it exists, and clarifying next steps with integrity.

Leaders model trust repair when they:

- Acknowledge mistakes without shifting blame
- Communicate rationale behind decisions with openness
- Listen actively to affected stakeholders
- Follow through consistently on commitments

When accountability is visible, credibility begins to rebuild.

 **Structural or Cultural Reinforcement: Institutionalize Repair Practices**

Trust repair cannot rely solely on individual leadership charisma or goodwill. Institutions must embed relational accountability into their systems.

Identify one structural practice that supports trust rebuilding, such as:

- Creating formal feedback and listening channels
- Establishing restorative dialogue processes
- Reviewing decision-making transparency protocols
- Building regular opportunities for community input

When repair is built into institutional practice, trust becomes renewable rather than fragile.

> ## Leadership Anchor: Restore Trust Through Responsibility, Not Reputation
>
> Trust is not restored through polished messaging or reputation management. It is rebuilt through consistent responsibility, honest engagement, and sustained relational care. Leaders who prioritize repair over image create cultures where accountability strengthens credibility rather than threatening authority. When responsibility becomes the foundation of leadership behavior, trust has space to grow again.

## Partnership as Leadership Architecture

Trust fractures quietly but heals visibly. Silence after an impact increases relational distance and damages credibility. Partnership promotes transparency before reputational strain turns into distrust. Repair is stronger when accountability is shared rather than defended.

## Part II Synthesis

### Leading With Emotional Integrity Under Pressure

If Part I describes the state of contemporary educational leadership, Part II focuses on how leaders fit within it.

This section focuses on a leadership trait that is often misunderstood and seldom taught: emotional integrity. Not as personality, temperament, or emotional display — but as disciplined professional steadiness. Emotional integrity is the ability to stay grounded, relationally responsible, and internally consistent while managing pressure, conflict, reform cycles, and institutional change.

Across these chapters, a consistent leadership pattern has emerged. Effective leaders neither avoid emotion nor absorb it indiscriminately. They anchor themselves. They coach without crushing. They hold space without surrendering structure. They repair trust without retreating into authority or defensiveness. They remain present without becoming porous.

In this new perspective, strength appears different from how it is viewed in many traditional leadership models.

Strength is not about emotional suppression; it is about emotional steadiness.

Strength is not control through fear; it is influence built on trust.

Strength is not limitless endurance; it is being present with boundaries.

Part II challenges the quiet assumption that professionalism demands emotional distance. Instead, it argues that sustainable leadership requires emotional clarity — a disciplined awareness of what belongs to the leader, what belongs to the system, and what must be shared.

Yet a deeper truth has emerged as well: emotional integrity cannot be maintained as a lone achievement. When stability depends solely on one person's ability, it eventually breaks down under constant pressure. Emotional integrity becomes lasting only when leadership culture supports it — when reflection is normal, accountability is shared, communication is honest, and the responsibility for relational repair is spread out rather than centralized.

When institutions embed these practices, emotional integrity shifts from being exceptional to expected. It becomes part of the operating design rather than the responsibility of a particularly self-aware leader.

As leaders develop this discipline, the culture around them begins to recalibrate. Conversations become more honest without turning toxic. Feedback shifts from being defensive to being helpful. Conflict becomes manageable instead of destabilizing. Trust turns into something that can be repaired rather than fragile. Authority becomes more stable because it is no longer inflated by emotional overreaction.

But emotional integrity alone does not resolve structural misalignment.

A leader can remain grounded and still operate within a system influenced by inequality, cultural division, or concentrated responsibilities. Presence without redistribution only temporarily stabilizes tension. Awareness without structural change extends imbalance.

This is where the work must expand.

Part III builds on the internal discipline of emotional integrity and extends outward into collective leadership practice. It examines how emotionally grounded leaders shape culture, manage differences, and share responsibility across teams and institutions. It shifts focus from individual integrity to the flexibility of the collective.

Part II strengthened the leader's center.

Part III widens the circle of leadership — moving from anchored presence to shared design.

# PART III

## CULTURAL FLEXIBILITY ACROSS EDUCATIONAL SYSTEMS

### Cultural Flexibility in University Systems

If emotional integrity anchors leadership internally, cultural flexibility determines how that leadership engages difference externally.

Universities are microcosms of global diversity. Within a single institution, leaders navigate international faculty expectations, student activism, generational shifts in academic culture, disciplinary silos, community politics, and competing interpretations of institutional mission. Authority in these spaces is negotiated rather than imposed. Cultural missteps are amplified quickly, and relational fractures spread quietly.

Cultural flexibility in higher education is not aspirational. It is survival-level leadership competence. Leaders who lack it often experience escalating resistance, fragmented departments, disengaged faculty, and polarized campuses. Leaders who cultivate it build trust across ideological and generational lines, strengthen institutional relevance, and create environments that can endure complexity without splintering.

The principles explored in this section apply directly to faculty governance structures, community partnerships, equity initiatives, and cross-cultural collaboration within university systems. Cultural flexibility protects influence in environments where authority alone cannot secure alignment.

## Cultural Flexibility Inside the School Walls

Schools and educational institutions do not operate in a culturally neutral manner. They are shaped by generational values, community histories, social identities, professional norms, and evolving expectations about authority, equity, and belonging. Leaders are not only managing instruction and policy; they are navigating overlapping cultural realities that often collide within the same building.

Part III examines what happens when leadership fails to account for these realities—and what becomes possible when it does.

Cultural flexibility is not the abandonment of standards nor an attempt to appease every voice. It is disciplined responsiveness. It is the capacity to recognize differences without defensiveness, to interpret behavior in context rather than through assumptions, and to adapt leadership approaches without sacrificing coherence or authority.

In today's schools and universities, cultural tension rarely manifests in overt conflict. It appears in subtler forms: generational misunderstandings framed as attitude problems, community conflict misread as defiance, equity efforts experienced as divisive rather than inclusive, and inclusion work disproportionately carried by the same individuals. When leaders respond through enforcement rather than interpretation, escalation replaces resolution, and compliance replaces commitment.

This section explores how cultural dynamics function not as abstract theory but as lived leadership challenges that shape morale, retention, credibility, and trust.

## Beyond One-Size-Fits-All Leadership

Many traditional leadership models assume uniformity—that expectations, communication styles, and motivational approaches will have a consistent impact across staff and communities. In reality, educational institutions are among the most culturally layered organizations in society.

Veteran educators and early-career teachers often operate from fundamentally different professional narratives. Faculty from varying cultural and community backgrounds may interpret institutional decisions through distinct lenses of power and trust. Parents and communities bring historical experiences that shape their responses long before policies are explained.

Cultural flexibility enables leaders to acknowledge these differences without fracturing cohesion. It does not dilute shared goals. Instead, it refines how those goals are communicated, sequenced, and supported so alignment becomes relational rather than forced.

## Equity Without Fracture

Equity leadership is one of the most emotionally complex responsibilities in contemporary education. When approached without cultural awareness, it can unintentionally deepen division, exhaust underrepresented staff, and trigger backlash that undermines its purpose.

Cultural flexibility invites leaders to hold multiple emotional realities simultaneously. It requires acknowledging fear, fatigue, and resistance without centering them. It requires promoting inclusion without isolating the very individuals the work intends to protect. It demands awareness of how implementation is experienced differently across positional identities within the institution.

Equity becomes destabilizing only when its emotional labor is centralized. It becomes transformative when its responsibility is shared.

## Inclusion as Structural Responsibility

In many institutions, inclusion efforts rely repeatedly on the same individuals—often those from marginalized backgrounds—to educate, interpret, advocate, and absorb emotional tension. Over time, this dynamic produces tokenism fatigue and quiet disengagement.

Cultural flexibility challenges this pattern. It reframes inclusion not as volunteerism but as architecture. Leadership must intentionally redistribute the labor of belonging across the system. When inclusion is embedded structurally rather than personified, it stabilizes culture instead of exhausting contributors.

Shared responsibility protects both people and the mission.

## A Bridge Between Integrity and Identity

Part III connects emotional integrity with identity agility. Cultural flexibility requires leaders to examine their own assumptions, positional authority, and default leadership posture. It calls for awareness of how personal identity shapes professional presence and how institutional design amplifies or constrains certain voices.

The chapters that follow address generational tension, community context, equity navigation, and inclusive team-building without reducing or performing. They present a leadership stance grounded in humility, clarity, and adaptability.

In environments characterized by difference, rigidity accelerates division. Flexibility creates alignment.

In educational systems under sustained strain, that distinction defines endurance.

## From Difference to Design

Culture is never neutral. It is shaped daily through decision pathways, relational tone, voice distribution, and the invisible hierarchies that determine whose experience defines normal. What appears organic is often the product of accumulated design.

Cultural flexibility is not passive tolerance. It is a disciplined adaptation without identity erasure. It requires navigating generational tensions, community expectations, and equity complexities without isolating individuals or fragmenting teams. It demands humility paired with structural awareness.

Yet culture cannot be stewarded by a single leader.

When inclusion efforts concentrate emotional labor on those already carrying disproportionate weight, fatigue deepens rather than resolves. When a difference is misinterpreted as resistance instead of context, fragmentation accelerates. Cultural complexity destabilizes systems only when responsibility for holding it remains centralized.

Partnership transforms cultural tension into shared design. It shifts inclusion from initiative to infrastructure. Culture evolves not when a single leader adapts more skillfully, but when systems are structured to hold differences without fracture.

## Partnership Lens

Culture does not shift through intention alone; it shifts through shared design. What appears as conflict is often concentrated responsibility. Inclusion strengthens when emotional labor is redistributed before fatigue hardens into withdrawal. Cultural flexibility becomes durable when leadership is shared rather than centralized.

# CHAPTER 9

## GENERATIONAL TENSION BETWEEN VETERAN AND NEW EDUCATORS

**Global Leadership Spotlight**

**Country Focus: Germany**
**Generational Workforce Tension**

Germany's education system is undergoing a major workforce shift as many experienced teachers are nearing retirement while younger educators are entering the field. National education authorities have recognized teacher shortages in certain regions and subject areas, putting pressure on efforts to quickly recruit, train, and retain new teachers. This demographic change has brought new challenges to school leadership and staff culture.

Differences in professional expectations, communication styles, and work-life boundaries often appear across generations. Veteran educators may bring extensive institutional knowledge and established norms, while newer educators often seek greater flexibility, collaborative leadership, and clearer boundaries around workload. Without deliberate leadership strategies, these differences can be mistaken for attitude issues or resistance instead of cultural differences.

Germany's experience underscores a broader leadership lesson: generational tension is often rooted in cultural differences, not personal conflicts. Adaptive leaders understand that workforce transitions require intentional bridge-building. By fostering spaces for mutual learning, defining shared values, and establishing inclusive professional norms, leaders can turn generational diversity into a source of organizational strength instead of division.

**Leadership Reflection:**

How do leadership practices in your organization acknowledge generational differences while building shared expectations and collective responsibility?

Generational tension in schools is rarely about age.

It is about meaning.

Across K–12 schools and higher education institutions, leaders are increasingly mediating conflicts between experienced educators and newer staff. This tension is often oversimplified: older staff are seen as resistant to change, while younger staff are seen as lacking commitment. However, these narratives are convenient—but profoundly misleading.

What appears to be an attitude is often a clash of assumptions, shaped by different professional backgrounds, economic realities, and cultural norms. When leaders misunderstand these tensions, they respond with correction instead of understanding, leading to escalation rather than alignment.

This chapter explores how generational differences in commitment, communication, and expectations unfold within educational systems—and why leadership, rather than personality, determines whether those differences cause division or foster growth.

## Different Definitions of Commitment

Veteran educators often define commitment through longevity, consistency, and sacrifice. Many entered the profession during a time when stability, institutional loyalty, and long-term service were key components of professional identity. Staying late, taking on extra responsibilities, and putting work above personal boundaries were not just common—they were signs of dedication.

Newer educators, by contrast, often define commitment in terms of sustainability, effectiveness, and alignment. They may focus on setting boundaries, challenging inefficient practices, and opposing narratives that equate exhaustion with excellence. Their commitment isn't necessarily weaker—it's simply expressed differently.

When these definitions clash, misunderstandings occur. Veteran educators might see newer colleagues as disengaged or not committed enough. New educators may view veteran norms as outdated or unhealthy. Both views overlook the deeper truth: each group is acting logically given the conditions it faced when entering the profession.

Leaders who fail to recognize these different frameworks risk strengthening division. Leaders who acknowledge them can help teams express shared values without requiring uniformity.

## Communication Norms as Cultural Markers

Communication style is one of the most visible—and volatile—sites of generational tension.

Veteran educators may favor face-to-face conversation, hierarchical channels, and implicit understanding developed over time. Newer educators may rely more heavily on written communication, direct questioning, and explicit clarification of expectations. What one group experiences as professionalism, another may experience as distance or rigidity.

These differences are often misunderstood as disrespect or insubordination. A direct question is seen as a challenge. A preference for documentation is interpreted as mistrust. Silence is regarded either as agreement or disengagement, depending on the perspective.

Leaders are crucial in translating these norms. Without leadership, communication differences are minimized. With intentional leadership, they are negotiated.

Effective leaders clearly define norms. They set expectations for communication without favoring any one style. They demonstrate curiosity rather than assumptions and establish shared agreements that reduce friction without eliminating differences.

## The Attitude Misdiagnosis

Perhaps the most damaging aspect of generational tension is how quickly it is attributed to attitude.

When newer educators question their workload, ask for clarity, or set boundaries, they are often labeled as difficult. When experienced educators express skepticism about new initiatives, they are seen as resistant. In both cases, complex cultural dynamics are oversimplified as personal flaws.

This misdiagnosis enables leadership to ignore systemic issues. Workload stays the same. Communication remains unclear. Initiative overload persists. The problem is seen as a people issue rather than a design problem.

Attitude labels hide the real questions leaders should ask. What assumptions are in conflict? Which values feel threatened? What experiences have influenced these reactions? And how might leadership structures be creating division instead of unity?

When leaders shift from judgment to interpretation, generational tension becomes informative rather than inflammatory.

## Leadership as Cultural Interpreter

Generational diversity, when led poorly, fragments teams. When led well, it strengthens them.

Leaders serve as cultural interpreters—helping educators understand not only what is being asked, but also why different responses exist. This does not mean excusing unprofessional behavior or abandoning shared standards. It involves framing behavior in context so it can be addressed constructively.

Interpretive leadership involves acknowledging differences without exaggeration. It involves validating concerns without solidifying positions. It involves maintaining a shared purpose while permitting different paths to achieve it.

Leaders who avoid this work often resort to favoritism—either defending veteran norms at the expense of innovation or prioritizing new voices without respecting institutional memory. Both methods increase resentment.

Cultural flexibility requires leaders to balance both continuity and change without letting one override the other.

## Bridging Without Forcing Uniformity

The goal of addressing generational tension is not consensus on every norm. It is functional alignment.

Schools do not need educators to think identically. They need educators to understand each other well enough to collaborate without ongoing conflict. This requires leadership that rejects false binaries and instead promotes shared language around commitment, professionalism, and care.

When leaders view generational differences as strengths rather than issues, teams gain access to a wider perspective. Veteran educators provide depth, context, and long-term vision. Newer educators contribute innovation, questioning, and awareness of sustainability. Both are essential for institutions navigating rapid change.

## The Cost of Avoidance

When generational tension is ignored, it does not fade. It calcifies.

Teams become divided along unseen lines. Collaboration turns hesitant. Mentorship diminishes. Turnover rises—not because educators cannot work together, but because leadership has failed to create conditions where differences can coexist without judgment.

Avoidance also deepens silence. Educators stop naming tension because they believe it won't be addressed thoughtfully. This silence further solidifies misunderstanding.

Leadership that avoids generational tension forfeits an opportunity for cultural coherence.

## Toward Generationally Intelligent Leadership

Generational intelligence is not about knowing stereotypes or superficially adapting language. It is about understanding how context shapes expectation—and how leadership decisions either widen or narrow those gaps.

This chapter encourages leaders to go beyond attitude-based explanations and focus on context-aware leadership. It urges leaders to assess how policies, communication practices, and cultural norms might favor one definition of commitment over others.

Generational tension is not evidence of decline.

It is evidence of transition.

Leaders who approach it with rigidity will deepen division. Leaders who approach it with cultural flexibility can transform tension into learning, friction into clarity, and difference into strength.

The chapters that follow will continue this work—examining community context, equity navigation, and inclusive team-building—each requiring the same foundational skill: the ability to lead across difference without losing cohesion.

That is the work of culturally flexible leadership.

# INSIDE THE CLASSROOM

## When Generations Collide Quietly

During a team planning meeting, a younger teacher suggested using a new digital platform to make grading and feedback easier. A veteran colleague crossed their arms and sighed loudly. No words were spoken, but the tension was clear immediately.

Later, in the hallway, the younger teacher admitted feeling dismissed. The veteran teacher, speaking separately, expressed frustration at being constantly asked to "change the way they had always done things." Both felt unheard and disrespected. Neither intended harm.

What unfolded was not about technology. It was about identity, belonging, and differing definitions of professionalism shaped by generational experience.

Without intentional leadership, these moments can turn into assumptions. Innovation is often labeled as arrogance. Experience can be seen as resistance. Cultural flexibility requires leaders to recognize these underlying currents and create space for mutual understanding instead of silent division.

---

## LEADERSHIP NEXT STEPS — Generational Workforce Tension

 **Awareness Shift: Recognize Generational Tension as a System Design Issue**

Generational conflict is often framed as a clash of attitudes or work ethics. In reality, it is frequently the result of structural misalignment — different entry conditions, evolving professional expectations, and uneven support systems across career stages.

Begin reframing generational tension as a leadership design challenge rather than a personality problem. Notice where policies, workload distribution, communication norms, or evaluation practices unintentionally favor one group over another.

**Ask yourself:**

Where has institutional design amplified generational friction instead of supporting collaboration?

 **Leadership Behavior Adjustment: Facilitate Mutual Understanding Without Stereotyping**

Leaders play a critical role in shaping how generations perceive one another. When leaders tolerate stereotypes or dismiss concerns as generational weakness, division deepens. Effective leadership requires facilitating dialogue that builds mutual respect without reinforcing assumptions.

Leaders support generational alignment when they:

- Acknowledge different professional realities without ranking value
- Create space for shared learning between experience levels
- Address conflict directly rather than allowing resentment to grow
- Communicate expectations with clarity across generational norms

When leaders model respect across generations, collaboration becomes possible rather than competitive.

 **Structural or Cultural Reinforcement: Build Intergenerational Collaboration Systems**

Sustainable workforce cohesion does not emerge spontaneously. It must be intentionally designed. Without structural support, generational differences often become fault lines rather than assets.

Identify one system-level practice that strengthens intergenerational collaboration, such as:

- Creating mentorship and reverse-mentorship programs
- Designing mixed-experience leadership teams
- Aligning onboarding and induction practices across cohorts
- Standardizing communication protocols that reduce generational misinterpretation

When collaboration is structurally supported, generational diversity becomes a leadership advantage rather than a liability.

## Leadership Anchor: Lead Across Difference Without Dividing the Workforce

Generational diversity reflects evolving professional realities, not leadership failure. Sustainable leaders resist the temptation to choose sides or reinforce narratives of superiority. Instead, they create environments where experience and innovation coexist. When leaders model respect, curiosity, and shared purpose, generational differences become sources of strength rather than division.

## Partnership as Leadership Architecture

Generational differences are about context, not character flaws. When interpretation relies on a single authority, tension turns into conflict. Partnership fosters shared understanding across different experience levels and career stages. Culture becomes stronger when differences are viewed as a collective effort rather than personal frustration.

# CHAPTER 10

## CULTURAL AND COMMUNITY CONTEXTS SHAPING THE SCHOOLHOUSE

### Global Leadership Spotlight

**Country Focus: India**
**Cultural and Community Contexts Shaping Schools**

India's education system caters to one of the most linguistically, culturally, and socioeconomically diverse student populations in the world. With hundreds of languages spoken across regions and significant differences in resource access between urban and rural areas, educational leadership in India must continuously adapt to local contexts. National reforms, including the National Education Policy (NEP 2020), emphasize multilingual education, community involvement, flexible learning options, and regionally responsive implementation strategies.

School leaders must balance national curriculum standards with local realities. This involves managing differences in family expectations, cultural norms, economic conditions, and community priorities. In many cases, leaders also collaborate closely with local stakeholders to tackle attendance, access, and infrastructure issues while upholding academic standards.

This environment teaches a broader global leadership lesson: culture is not just an external factor that leadership circumvents—it is the environment in which leadership functions. Effective leaders cultivate cultural flexibility by listening to community voices, adapting practices to local needs, and respecting diverse identities without undermining institutional goals. When leadership remains inflexible, misalignment arises. When leadership adapts thoughtfully, trust and engagement grow.

**Leadership Reflection:**

What assumptions about "normal" schooling might need to shift in order to better reflect and serve the cultural realities of your community?

Schools do not exist outside culture.

They sit within it, respond to it, and are shaped by it—often in ways leaders are expected to navigate quietly and flawlessly.

Every school operates at the intersection of many value systems: those of families, communities, institutions, governing bodies, and the larger social context. These systems don't always match up. In fact, they often conflict—placing educators and leaders in the role of mediators between expectations that can't be fully aligned.

This chapter explores how cultural and community contexts shape the emotional environment of schools and institutions, and how leaders bear the burden of managing conflicting values without adequate acknowledgment or support.

## Community Expectations as Invisible Pressure

Community expectations exert constant influence on schools, even when they are not explicitly voiced. Families bring beliefs about discipline, rigor, equity, communication, and authority.

Communities carry historical relationships with educational institutions—some grounded in trust, others shaped by exclusion, disappointment, or harm.

Leaders are expected to understand and respond to these expectations intuitively. When expectations align with institutional norms, leadership feels straightforward. When they conflict, leaders must make decisions that inevitably leave some groups dissatisfied.

This tension is often described as public relations or stakeholder management. In reality, it is emotional labor—work that requires leaders to absorb frustration, fear, and anger while maintaining relational composure.

Over time, the pressure to meet conflicting expectations can create internal stress. Leaders may feel pulled in opposite directions, trying to protect staff while satisfying community demands, or defending institutional decisions while addressing legitimate concerns. This balancing act is rarely seen, but it deeply influences leadership ability.

## Cultural Misunderstandings and Their Consequences

Cultural misunderstandings come not only from differences but also from assumptions. When leaders interpret behavior through their own cultural lens without enough context, misunderstandings occur.

A family's silence might be seen as disengagement instead of respect. A teacher's directness could be interpreted as disrespect rather than urgency. A community's resistance might be seen as an obstruction rather than a historical caution.

These misinterpretations are rarely deliberate. They occur when leaders are under pressure to respond quickly, with little time to consider context or develop relational understanding. However, the consequences can be significant.

Cultural misunderstandings quietly weaken trust. They reinforce stereotypes and unnecessarily escalate conflicts. Often, they leave educators—especially those from marginalized backgrounds—feeling unseen or unfairly judged.

Leaders lacking cultural flexibility tend to enforce policies rather than ask questions. Those who develop cultural awareness take the time to consider what might be influencing their observed responses.

## Conflicting Value Systems Inside the Same Walls

One of the most emotionally taxing aspects of educational leadership is navigating conflicting value systems within the same institution.

Schools are asked to be rigorous and compassionate, neutral and values-driven, consistent and adaptable. Educators are expected to uphold institutional standards while addressing individual student needs. Leaders must interpret policies through the lenses of equity, legality, and community expectations—often simultaneously.

These conflicts do not have clean resolutions. Choosing one value often means disappointing another.

When leaders lack space to acknowledge this complexity, they internalize it. Decisions become personal burdens rather than shared institutional challenges. Leaders might feel isolated and question their judgment or values when they are actually dealing with irreconcilable demands.

This emotional toll accumulates over time. It can manifest as decision paralysis, emotional withdrawal, or chronic self-doubt—not because leaders lack conviction, but because they are holding tensions no single individual can resolve alone.

## The Emotional Cost of Being the Intermediary

Educational leaders often serve as mediators—translating between systems that use different cultural languages. They clarify institutional constraints to communities, community staffing needs, and policy mandates to all involved.

This role demands continuous emotional adjustment. Leaders must remain empathetic without taking any one stance. They need to communicate clearly without increasing tension. They must manage dissatisfaction without fighting back or pulling away.

Yet this intermediary role is rarely recognized as emotionally demanding. Leaders are expected to handle it smoothly, as if staying neutral were effortless rather than challenging.

When this labor goes unrecognized, leaders may start to feel unnoticed themselves. They carry the emotional burden of conflict well after discussions end, often without support from peers or validation from the institution.

## Cultural Flexibility as Leadership Capacity

Cultural flexibility doesn't require agreement with every viewpoint or the avoidance of tough choices. Instead, it involves understanding that behavior is influenced by context—and that effective leadership depends on grasping that context before taking action.

Culturally flexible leaders avoid simple explanations. They consider how history, identity, and power dynamics may influence current interactions. They take time to interpret situations carefully to prevent unnecessary escalation.

This approach does not weaken authority. It strengthens legitimacy.

When communities feel understood—even if decisions don't match their preferences—trust can grow. When educators acknowledge cultural context rather than ignore it, engagement rises. When leaders demonstrate curiosity rather than certainty, they foster collaboration rather than resistance.

## When Culture Is Ignored

Ignoring cultural and community context does not simplify leadership. It makes it more brittle.

Leaders who rely solely on policy enforcement may achieve compliance but lose relational trust. Leaders who dismiss community emotion as irrational may preserve efficiency but deepen division. Leaders who avoid cultural complexity altogether often find themselves managing repeated conflict rather than addressing root causes.

Cultural rigidity increases emotional strain for everyone involved. It narrows options, escalates misunderstanding, and concentrates emotional labor at the top.

## Leading Within, Not Above, Culture

This chapter does not imply that leaders must resolve all cultural conflicts. It suggests that leaders must stop pretending they are above it.

Schools are cultural spaces. Leadership is cultural work.

When leaders openly acknowledge this—by naming conflicting values, clarifying constraints, and engaging difference with humility—they lessen the emotional burden of uncertainty. They demonstrate integrity not by having all the answers, but by navigating complexity with steadiness and respect.

Cultural and community contexts will continue to shape the school environment. The question is whether leaders engage with them thoughtfully or defensively, flexibly or rigidly.

The upcoming chapters will expand on this foundation by exploring how leaders handle equity, inclusion, and shared responsibility within culturally complex systems.

Because lasting leadership does not dismiss culture.

It understands it well enough to lead from within—without sacrificing coherence, compassion, or credibility.

# INSIDE THE CLASSROOM

## The Meeting That Meant Different Things

A community meeting was called to address concerns about new discipline procedures. Families filled the room, each bringing different expectations shaped by culture, history, and lived experience.

One parent spoke passionately about fairness. Another stressed safety. A third asked whether the school truly understood the community it served.

The administrator noticed how the same policy language landed differently across the room. What felt neutral on paper carried emotional weight in practice.

After the meeting, a teacher commented, "I didn't realize how differently this was being received." It was not ignorance. It was exposure.

Schools function within larger cultural systems. Leadership demands understanding that decisions are not made in isolation — they are influenced by community memory, values, and trust. Cultural flexibility starts with listening before defending.

---

## LEADERSHIP NEXT STEPS — Cultural and Community Contexts Shaping Schools

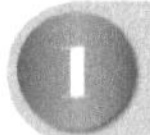 **Awareness Shift: Recognize Community Context as Leadership Reality**

Schools do not operate in isolation. They are shaped by the cultural histories, socioeconomic realities, values, and expectations of the communities they serve. When leaders attempt to apply standardized leadership approaches without attending to local context, disconnect and mistrust often follow.

Begin viewing community context not as a complication to manage, but as essential leadership information. Pay attention to family expectations, cultural norms, and historical relationships between institutions and communities. These dynamics shape how leadership decisions are received and interpreted.

**Ask yourself:**

Where am I making leadership decisions without fully accounting for community realities?

## Leadership Behavior Adjustment: Practice Culturally Responsive Leadership Presence

Culturally responsive leadership requires more than awareness. It demands humility, listening, and relational engagement. Leaders must learn to communicate across cultural differences without assuming shared norms or expectations.

Leaders demonstrate culturally responsive presence when they:

- Listen to community voices before implementing change
- Adapt communication styles to different cultural contexts
- Acknowledge historical mistrust where it exists
- Invite community participation in school decision-making

When leaders lead with cultural awareness, schools become more trusted and more effective.

## Structural or Cultural Reinforcement: Build Community-Integrated Leadership Systems

Sustainable community engagement cannot depend on individual leaders alone. Institutions must embed community connection into their leadership structures.

Identify one system-level adjustment that strengthens school–community alignment, such as:

- Establishing community advisory councils
- Creating formal family engagement roles or teams
- Integrating cultural competency training into leadership development
- Building regular feedback loops with families and local organizations

When community engagement is structurally supported, trust becomes institutional rather than individual.

---

## Leadership Anchor: Lead With the Community, Not Above It

Effective school leadership is not exercised over communities — it is practiced alongside them. Leaders who position themselves as partners rather than authorities create conditions for mutual trust, shared ownership, and collective responsibility. When leadership is grounded in relationship and respect, schools become more responsive, resilient, and culturally connected.

## Partnership as Leadership Architecture 

Conflicting value systems call for dialogue, not dominance. Authority alone cannot resolve cultural tensions without making them worse. Partnership spreads the effort of building understanding across the organization so no single voice controls what is normal. Stability happens when differences are managed together.

# CHAPTER 11
## CULTURAL FLEXIBILITY IN PARENT, TEACHER, AND COMMUNITY RELATIONSHIPS

Mexico's education system has increasingly focused on family engagement and community partnerships as key elements of student success. National education initiatives have emphasized schools' role as community hubs, promoting stronger collaboration among educators, parents, and local organizations. In many areas, school leaders are expected to coordinate outreach efforts, improve communication channels, and build trust with families who may face economic, linguistic, or access barriers.

These efforts mirror a broader leadership truth: schools don't function in isolation. Student learning is influenced by relationships that extend beyond the classroom. When leaders focus on transparent communication, cultural humility, and ongoing engagement with families, they foster shared responsibility for educational results.

Neglecting relationships leads to misunderstandings, loss of trust, and diminished institutional credibility.

Mexico's experience highlights the value of relational bridges. Leadership that focuses on connection does not replace academic rigor; it enhances it by aligning school expectations with community realities. Sustainable improvement relies on partnerships, not isolation.

**Leadership Reflection:**

How does your institution intentionally build trust, communication, and shared responsibility with families and community stakeholders?

Leadership in education requires more than clear communication. It requires translation.

Schools and institutions communicate through policies, procedures, and professional norms. Families and communities express themselves through lived experiences, emotions, and deeply held values. When leaders believe that clarity alone can close this gap, misunderstandings happen.

Translation differs from explanation. The explanation shows what is happening. Translation helps people see why it matters to them, how it fits their worldview, and what it demands of their trust. Without translation, even carefully crafted messages can seem dismissive, threatening, or unclear.

This chapter examines how culturally flexible leadership manifests in relationships with parents, teachers, and communities, especially when frustration spikes and values clash.

## Navigating Parent Frustration Without Escalation

Parent frustration is often seen as hostility or entitlement. In truth, it more often stems from fear—fear for a child's well-being, future, or acceptance within an institution. When leaders react to frustration defensively or bureaucratically, that fear only grows.

Effective leaders learn to separate emotion from attack. They listen for concern beneath the tone and resist the impulse to justify before understanding. This doesn't mean conceding authority or abandoning standards. It means recognizing that frustration is often a request for reassurance, not a challenge to leadership legitimacy.

When leaders recognize parent emotion without immediately trying to fix it, they create space for de-escalation. Frustration lessens when people feel heard. Even if outcomes don't change, relational trust remains through respectful engagement.

## Cultural Humility in Conflict

Conflict across cultural lines requires humility—not as self-diminishment, but as disciplined openness.

Cultural humility starts with recognizing that leaders experience institutions differently from families and educators. Historical exclusion, systemic inequities, and past harm influence how policies and interactions are seen. Ignoring this context doesn't keep neutrality; it favors dominant perspectives.

In moments of conflict, culturally flexible leaders pause their interpretation. They ask what might be influencing the response they are seeing. They avoid assuming intent and stay open to learning—even when the conversation feels uncomfortable.

Humility does not require leaders to absorb blame or accept mischaracterization. It requires them to stay engaged without becoming defensive. This stance allows leaders to hold authority while signaling respect.

## Translation Across Professional and Community Cultures

Teachers and families often have different assumptions about education. Educators might focus on developmental pacing, institutional constraints, and collective outcomes. Families may emphasize individual needs, immediate impact, and personal experiences.

Leaders who expect alignment without a clear explanation set everyone up for frustration. Cultural flexibility requires leaders to clearly communicate not only what decisions are being made, but how those decisions align—or clash—with community values.

Translation involves framing expectations in ways that resonate across cultures. It means explaining institutional limits without hiding behind them. It means naming trade-offs honestly and acknowledging where systems fall short.

When leaders communicate effectively, they decrease suspicion. They help stakeholders understand the reasoning behind decisions, even if they disagree with the outcomes.

## Building Relational Bridges Without Self-Betrayal

One of the biggest challenges in culturally complex leadership is keeping integrity while forming connections.

Leaders might feel pressured to appease, over-accommodate, or soften boundaries to keep peace. Over time, this can cause self-betrayal—where leaders agree just to preserve relationships but end up losing clarity, consistency, or credibility.

Cultural flexibility doesn't mean leaders must abandon their values or professional judgment. Instead, it involves communicating those values in ways that are respectful, transparent, and rooted in relationships.

Healthy boundaries are vital for sustainable leadership. Leaders who regularly bend to avoid conflict end up causing confusion rather than building trust. Leaders who set boundaries with empathy foster predictability—an essential part of relational safety.

## When Translation Is Absent

When translation does not occur, frustration escalates. Parents feel dismissed. Educators feel undermined. Leaders feel caught in the middle, absorbing conflict without resolution.

Over time, this dynamic erodes trust on all sides. Communication becomes reactive. Relationships become transactional. Cultural misunderstandings harden into assumptions.

Leaders may begin to withdraw emotionally, limiting engagement to what feels manageable. This withdrawal further distances communities and reinforces cycles of mistrust.

## Leadership as Relational Interpreter

Culturally adaptable leaders see their role not as referees or enforcers, but as relational interpreters. They help different groups hear each other without distorting meaning. They recognize emotions without escalating conflict. They keep coherence without requiring conformity.

This work requires emotional steadiness, cultural awareness, and ethical clarity. It is not glamorous, and it is rarely recognized. Yet it is central to leadership in diverse educational environments.

Translation is labor. It takes time, attention, and skill. When leaders are supported in this work, relationships deepen and trust strengthens. When leaders are left to navigate it alone, fatigue grows.

## Leading Without Losing Yourself

This chapter does not imply that leaders should constantly absorb frustration or sacrifice themselves to preserve harmony. Instead, it emphasizes that cultural flexibility should be combined with emotional integrity.

Leaders can listen without conceding. They can empathize without internalizing blame. They can build bridges without abandoning their role.

In strained educational systems, relational leadership is essential. However, it must be practiced in ways that safeguard both the leader and the community.

The upcoming chapters will continue to explore how leaders handle equity work, inclusion, and shared responsibility—each requiring the same core skill: the ability to lead across differences with clarity, humility, and steadiness.

Leadership involves translating, not just communicating. And when done with integrity, translation enables schools and institutions to embrace differences without breaking apart—strengthening the relationships that support learning itself.

# INSIDE THE CLASSROOM

## The Conversation That Needed Translation

A parent-teacher conference quickly became tense. The teacher highlighted academic expectations, while the parent emphasized emotional wellbeing. Both wanted the student to succeed but felt misunderstood.

The administrator stepped in and redirected the conversation. They began by stating the shared goal. Then they expressed concerns without blaming anyone. The tone became gentler. The conversation moved in a new direction.

What changed was not the issue. It was the language.

Leadership in culturally diverse environments often calls for translation, not mediation. It involves helping people understand each other despite differences in communication styles, values, and expectations.

Bridges are built through understanding, not assumption.

---

## LEADERSHIP NEXT STEPS —<br>Family and Community Relationships

 **Awareness Shift: Recognize Relationship Diversity as Leadership Complexity**

Family, teacher, and community relationships are shaped by cultural expectations, communication norms, and differing views of authority and partnership. When leaders apply a single relational approach across diverse communities, misunderstanding and conflict often follow.

Begin viewing relational diversity as a leadership complexity rather than a barrier. Pay attention to how cultural values influence expectations around communication, decision-making, and trust-building. These differences are not obstacles — they are leadership data.

**Ask yourself:**

Where am I relying on one communication style that may not resonate across cultures?

## Leadership Behavior Adjustment: Practice Adaptive Relationship Leadership

Cultural flexibility requires leaders to adjust how they communicate, listen, and respond across contexts without compromising professional boundaries or institutional standards. Adaptive leadership does not mean abandoning expectations. It means translating them in ways that respect cultural difference.

Leaders demonstrate adaptive relationship leadership when they:

- Modify communication approaches for different family and community contexts
- Clarify expectations using culturally accessible language
- Seek understanding before assuming resistance
- Balance institutional consistency with relational sensitivity

When leaders adapt relationally, trust becomes more attainable across differences.

###  Structural or Cultural Reinforcement: Institutionalize Cultural Responsiveness

Cultural flexibility cannot rely solely on individual leadership skills. Institutions must embed inclusive practices into their systems to sustain meaningful family and community engagement.

Identify one structural practice that strengthens culturally responsive relationships, such as:

- Providing multilingual communication resources
- Training staff in cross-cultural communication
- Establishing culturally representative advisory groups
- Revising engagement policies to reflect community diversity

When cultural responsiveness is institutionalized, relationship-building becomes sustainable rather than sporadic.

---

## Leadership Anchor:
## Build Trust Through Cultural Adaptability

Trust is not built through uniform leadership behavior. It grows when leaders demonstrate respect for differences while maintaining a clear purpose. Cultural adaptability allows leaders to remain consistent in their values while remaining flexible in their approach. When leaders meet families and communities where they are, relationships strengthen, and collaboration becomes possible.

## Partnership as Leadership Architecture

Relational bridges can't be built from just one office. Translation requires humility, patience, and shared ownership. Partnership broadens responsibility for trust-building across roles and relationships. Connection lasts when cultural navigation becomes a collective practice.

# CHAPTER 12

## NAVIGATING EQUITY WORK WITHOUT FRAGMENTING THE STAFF

**Global Leadership Spotlight**

**Country Focus: Brazil**
**Equity Work and Organizational Strain**

Brazil's education system continues to face deeply rooted racial, regional, and socioeconomic inequalities that impact access to quality education and student achievements. National policies and reform efforts aim to increase inclusion, lessen regional gaps, and address the historical exclusion of marginalized groups. These initiatives often require schools and teachers to adopt new practices focused on culturally responsive teaching, inclusive curriculum development, and community involvement.

While these reforms are essential, they often add emotional and administrative burdens on educators and school leaders. Frequently, a small group of dedicated staff members bear the responsibility for equity work without corresponding adjustments to workload, staffing, or resources. When equity efforts depend mainly on personal commitment instead of organizational change, they risk becoming unsustainable.

Brazil's experience underscores an important leadership lesson: equity work must be inherently supported to be sustainable. Lasting progress depends on a well-planned sequence of change, redistribution of responsibility, and alignment between policy goals and operational capacity. When leaders view equity as a core organizational priority rather than an individual burden, they safeguard both people and purpose.

**Leadership Reflection:**

How is equity work supported through staffing, time allocation, and institutional structures in your organization—and where does additional support need to be built?

E quity initiatives rarely fail due to a lack of moral clarity.

They often fail because they aren't emotionally prepared.

In schools and educational institutions, equity work is often approached with urgency and strong belief. The intention is good. The goals are important. However, leaders are often caught off guard when these efforts provoke division, defensiveness, or quiet withdrawal rather than unified participation.

This reaction is often mistaken for opposition to equity itself. In fact, it more often results from how the work is presented, paced, and emotionally managed. When leaders move too quickly for the system's emotional capacity, even well-planned equity efforts can undermine trust rather than strengthen it.

This chapter examines how culturally flexible leadership guides equity work without isolating staff, exhausting those already burdened, or provoking resistance that hinders progress.

## Resistance as Fear, Not Defiance

Resistance in equity conversations is often seen as an unwillingness to change. While that can sometimes be true, it is far more common for resistance to indicate fear—fear of being shamed, exposed, misunderstood, or made irrelevant.

Educators may be afraid of saying the wrong thing and being judged. They might worry about losing their professional credibility. They could fear that long-standing practices will be dismissed without proper context or care. In some cases, they may fear that their sense of professional stability is shifting faster than they can adapt to it.

When leaders respond to this fear with correction or moral pressure, resistance stiffens. People stop asking questions. They disengage publicly while retreating privately. The work continues in name, but not in spirit.

Leaders who recognize fear beneath resistance respond differently. They slow down interpretation. They distinguish between harm and discomfort. They create space for learning without condoning harmful behavior. In doing so, they preserve momentum without escalating division.

## The Emotional Sequencing of Change

Equity work is not only intellectual or procedural. It is emotional.

Change that challenges identity, power, or belonging must be sequenced thoughtfully. When leaders introduce equity initiatives without preparing staff emotionally, they place people in a position where compliance feels safer than engagement.

Emotional sequencing means focusing on readiness before making a demand. It involves recognizing that discomfort is a natural part of growth, but also understanding that too much discomfort introduced too quickly can overwhelm instead of teach.

Leaders who sequence equity work effectively do not rush staff into action without providing context. They explain why the work matters, what it asks from people, and what support will be available along the way. They create space for questions without framing inquiry as resistance. They recognize that learning requires psychological safety as much as moral urgency.

This doesn't mean delaying equity forever. It means guiding it intentionally instead of reacting to it.

## The Hidden Cost to the Few

One of the most common—and least acknowledged—failures in equity work is the concentration of emotional labor.

Many institutions repeatedly rely on the same individuals to explain, advocate for, represent, and handle emotional reactions related to equity. Often, these individuals come from the very groups the work aims to support. Over time, this leads to exhaustion, resentment, and a feeling of being used rather than appreciated.

Leaders may believe they are amplifying voices when they are actually overburdening them.

Navigating equity work responsibly requires leaders to distribute emotional labor more evenly. This means making sure that responsibility for learning, reflection, and growth is shared across the organization—not placed on a few willing or visible individuals.

When leaders fail to address this imbalance, equity work becomes unsustainable. Those most committed to the work burn out, while others remain passive observers.

## Leading Without Polarizing

Equity work often becomes polarized when leaders frame it as a test of character rather than a process of growth. When people feel evaluated rather than invited, they retreat into defensiveness or silence.

Culturally flexible leaders resist binary framing. They avoid language that positions staff as either enlightened or problematic. Instead, they emphasize shared responsibility, ongoing learning, and collective accountability.

This approach does not dilute the seriousness of equity. It strengthens it by keeping people engaged rather than alienated.

Leaders who view equity as a professional practice rather than a moral sorting tool foster environments where tough conversations can occur without damaging trust.

## Integrity Without Isolation

Leaders often worry that slowing down or softening their tone will harm their integrity. In truth, integrity is broken when equity efforts damage community bonds or wear out participants.

Leading equity with integrity means holding firm to values while remaining responsive to people. It means refusing to sacrifice relationship for speed, or clarity for appeasement. It means recognizing that how the work is done communicates as much as what the work stands for.

When leaders model steadiness, humility, and accountability, they signal that equity is not a trend or a mandate, but a long-term commitment embedded in professional culture.

## Sustaining the Work Over Time

Equity is not implemented; it is cultivated.

Sustainable equity work requires leaders to revisit assumptions, monitor emotional impact, and adjust their approach without abandoning their purpose. It involves ongoing reflection on who is doing the work, how decisions are communicated, and where unintended harm might be happening.

This chapter does not provide a checklist for achieving equity. It offers a leadership orientation—one that treats emotion as part of the system rather than an obstacle to overcome.

Equity initiatives fail when they are emotionally unprepared.

They succeed when leaders address fear without losing clarity, pace change carefully, and shield the people doing the work from becoming collateral damage.

The chapters that follow will continue this exploration—examining how leaders build inclusive teams and distribute responsibility without burning out the few.

Because equity that divides the community is not true equity. And lasting leadership must know how to uphold both justice and humanity simultaneously.

# INSIDE THE CLASSROOM

## When Equity Work Feels Heavy

During a professional learning session on equity, the room felt tense. Some educators were engaged and passionate. Others sat quietly, arms crossed, unsure of what was expected or how safe it felt to speak.

A teacher later shared privately, "I support this work, but I'm afraid of saying the wrong thing." Another said, "It feels like more is being asked of the same few people."

The leader recognized the pattern: emotional readiness was uneven. The work was important, but the pacing and support structures mattered just as much as the content.

Equity leadership involves emotional sequencing — establishing psychological safety before asking for vulnerability, building trust before expecting transformation. Without this, even well-meaning initiatives can divide teams rather than unite them.

---

## LEADERSHIP NEXT STEPS —
## Equity Work and Organizational Strain

**Awareness Shift: Recognize Equity Tension as Organizational Stress, Not Individual Resistance**

Equity initiatives often surface deep emotions, historical wounds, and differing worldviews. When tension emerges, it is frequently interpreted as individual resistance or lack of commitment. In reality, much of this strain reflects organizational stress — the pressure created when values-based change is introduced without sufficient structure, dialogue, or shared understanding.

Begin reframing conflict around equity work as a leadership signal rather than a personnel problem. Notice where uncertainty, fear, or misalignment is being personalized instead of addressed collectively.

**Ask yourself:**

Where is equity-related tension being treated as individual failure instead of organizational strain?

 **Leadership Behavior Adjustment: Lead With Clarity, Courage, and Emotional Steadiness**

Equity leadership requires both moral clarity and emotional regulation. Leaders must communicate purpose without polarization and address discomfort without escalation. This demands steady presence, consistent messaging, and the ability to hold complexity without becoming reactive.

Leaders demonstrate this balance when they:

- Clearly articulate the purpose and scope of equity initiatives
- Set expectations for respectful dialogue and professional conduct
- Address misinformation without defensiveness
- Remain calm and grounded during emotionally charged conversations

When leaders model emotional steadiness, staff are more likely to remain engaged rather than divided.

 **Structural or Cultural Reinforcement: Design Inclusive Change Processes**

Equity work becomes destabilizing when it is implemented through top-down mandates without adequate participation or support. Sustainable progress requires inclusive structures that allow staff to engage, learn, and adapt together.

Identify one system-level adjustment that supports cohesive equity work, such as:

- Creating facilitated dialogue spaces for staff learning and reflection
- Establishing cross-role equity leadership teams
- Integrating equity goals into broader institutional priorities
- Providing professional development that supports skill-building rather than compliance

When equity initiatives are structurally supported, change becomes collaborative rather than fragmenting.

## Leadership Anchor: Advance Equity Without Sacrificing Unity

Equity leadership does not require choosing between justice and cohesion. Sustainable leaders hold both. They create space for difficult conversations while protecting relational integrity and professional respect. When leaders advance equity with clarity, steadiness, and inclusive process design, organizations can move forward without breaking apart.

## Partnership as Leadership Architecture 

Equity shouldn't rely on the emotional labor of only a few. When responsibility is concentrated, fatigue increases and fragmentation occurs. Partnership spreads advocacy and accountability throughout the system before stress isolates leaders. Inclusion becomes sustainable when stewardship is shared.

# CHAPTER 13

## BUILDING INCLUSIVE TEAMS WITHOUT BURNING OUT THE FEW

**Global Leadership Spotlight**

**Country Focus: Australia**
**Inclusion Without Burnout**

Australia's education sector has increasingly prioritized Indigenous inclusion, culturally responsive teaching, and reconciliation-driven education initiatives. National and state frameworks encourage schools to embed Indigenous perspectives into the curriculum, build stronger community partnerships, and address historical inequities in education. These efforts demonstrate a vital commitment to creating more inclusive learning environments.

At the school level, however, inclusion work is often performed by a small number of educators—often Indigenous staff members or those with strong equity expertise. These individuals may be asked to lead professional development, mediate cultural understanding, support students and families, and advise leadership teams, often in addition to their formal teaching or administrative duties. When this workload is not structurally recognized or evenly distributed, emotional fatigue and role strain tend to increase.

Australia's experience teaches a wider leadership lesson: inclusion cannot rely on just a few dedicated individuals. Sustainable inclusion needs shared responsibility, organizational support, and clear roles. When leaders intentionally assign equity responsibilities across teams, allocate time and resources, and embed inclusion into key organizational processes, they safeguard both people and progress.

**Leadership Reflection:**

Who carries the invisible emotional and relational labor in your organization—and how might leadership redistribute this work more equitably and sustainably?

In many schools and institutions, inclusion is sustained by the same people—again and again.

They are asked to serve on committees, mentor colleagues, represent diverse perspectives, mediate conflicts, and share their lived experiences. Their insight is valued. Their presence is appreciated. However, their labor is rarely protected. Over time, what begins as a contribution becomes an expectation, and expectation leads to exhaustion.

This chapter highlights a quiet but ongoing pattern in educational systems: the focus of inclusion efforts on a small group of people, often those from historically marginalized communities. While the goal may be recognition or trust, the result is often burnout, resentment, and withdrawal. Inclusion cannot be maintained when it depends on sacrifice instead of proper structure.

## The Weight of Invisible Labor

Much of the work that supports inclusive cultures is hidden. It does not show up in job descriptions, evaluation metrics, or workload assessments. It happens in conversations after meetings, in emotional translation between colleagues, in mentoring that goes beyond formal roles, and in the quiet efforts to make spaces safer for others.

This labor is often assumed rather than assigned. Leaders may not explicitly ask for it, yet systems depend on it. Over time, individuals bearing this burden feel recognized for their contribution but unnoticed in their capacity limits.

Invisible labor becomes especially draining when it is seen as a passion or a calling instead of work. When inclusion efforts depend only on goodwill, they become fragile, relying on the endurance of a few rather than the commitment of many.

## Tokenism Fatigue and the Cost of Representation

Tokenism fatigue occurs when people are repeatedly asked to represent an entire group, perspective, or identity. Even well-meaning invitations can become draining over time.

Representation becomes labor when it is not shared. Being "the voice" in the room requires constant vigilance—monitoring language, anticipating impact, and correcting missteps. It demands emotional regulation in spaces where one's identity is under discussion, often without adequate support.

Over time, tokenism fatigue leads to disengagement. Individuals may withdraw not because they no longer care, but because the cost of participation has become too high. When this occurs, institutions often interpret withdrawal as a lack of interest rather than a sign of overextension.

## When Inclusion Depends on Overfunctioning

Systems that depend on only a few people to handle inclusion create an imbalance that weakens their own objectives. Overworking some individuals leads to underperformance by others. Responsibility becomes unevenly shared, and inclusion shifts from being a systemic effort to a personal one.

Leaders may inadvertently reinforce this pattern by consistently turning to the same individuals for insight or leadership. While this can feel efficient, it prevents broader capacity-building and signals that inclusion is the responsibility of those most affected rather than a collective obligation.

Sustainable inclusion depends on leaders intentionally breaking this cycle.

## Structural Strategies for Shared Responsibility

Building inclusive teams without overburdening the few requires structural change, not just cultural affirmation. Leaders must create systems that embed inclusion into roles, processes, and expectations rather than add it through informal effort.

Shared responsibility starts with clarity. Inclusion efforts must be defined, funded, and allocated. Time, pay, and recognition should match the work being asked. When inclusion is seen as core work, it needs to be supported accordingly.

Leaders can also expand participation by creating shared learning structures. Instead of relying on individuals to teach peers informally, institutions can invest in collective professional development to establish a common language and understanding. This shifts the focus from explanation to engagement.

Rotating responsibility is another key strategy. Committees, task forces, and leadership roles related to inclusion should not always have the same members. Rotating membership broadens perspectives, enhances capacity, and demonstrates that inclusion is everyone's responsibility.

## Leadership Accountability in Inclusion Design

Leaders play a decisive role in whether inclusion becomes sustainable or extractive. This requires ongoing attention to who is being asked, how often, and at what cost.

Accountable leaders ask different questions. Who is carrying emotional labor that is not visible? Whose voices are consistently sought, and whose are absent? What systems are in place to protect those doing this work from overload?

Accountability also involves listening when individuals say no. Declining an invitation should not be interpreted as disengagement or lack of commitment. Often, it is a sign that capacity has been reached.

When leaders respond to these signals with respect rather than pressure, they preserve trust and signal that inclusion work will not come at the expense of well-being.

## From Symbolic Inclusion to Sustainable Practice

Inclusion becomes superficial when it depends on presence instead of process. Having diverse individuals in the room isn't the same as creating systems that enable diverse participation.

Sustainable inclusion requires leaders to move beyond representation toward responsibility. It asks leaders to examine how decisions are made, how conflict is addressed, and how accountability is shared.

When inclusion is embedded structurally, individuals are no longer asked to carry the work alone. The system itself begins to do the work it was designed to support.

## Protecting People While Advancing Purpose

This chapter does not advocate for less inclusion work. It advocates for better leadership of it.

Leaders who support those doing inclusion work preserve the integrity of the work itself. When emotional labor is recognized, shared, and backed, inclusion becomes a collective effort rather than an individual burden.

The same people should not always be asked to carry the work.

When they are, systems fail quietly.

The upcoming chapters will expand this discussion to include questions of identity, role changes, and collective care—each requiring the same core shift: leadership that creates sustainability rather than relying on sacrifice.

Inclusion based on exhaustion cannot last. Leadership that lasts must create teams where responsibility is shared, work is visible, and care is built into the structure — not optional.

# INSIDE THE CLASSROOM

## The Same Names, Every Time

When a new initiative was launched, the same staff members were asked to lead. They were capable. Trusted. Committed. And increasingly exhausted.

One teacher quietly declined the invitation this time. Not because they didn't care — but because they were tired of being the default.

Later, a colleague said, "It feels like inclusion work always lands on the same shoulders."

Invisible labor often goes unnoticed because it is normalized. Cultural flexibility requires leaders to recognize who is carrying the institution's emotional and relational work—and to redesign responsibilities so that inclusion does not become another source of burnout.

Shared leadership is not symbolic. It is structural.

---

## LEADERSHIP NEXT STEPS —
## Inclusion Without Burnout

### Awareness Shift: Recognize Invisible Labor as Organizational Risk

Inclusive initiatives often rely on a small group of highly engaged staff — frequently educators from marginalized backgrounds or those with strong advocacy identities. When inclusion work becomes concentrated on a few individuals, burnout becomes inevitable, and equity efforts lose sustainability.

Begin noticing where emotional, cultural, and relational labor is unevenly distributed. Pay attention to who is consistently asked to represent, mentor, translate, or lead inclusion efforts without formal recognition or workload adjustment. These patterns signal organizational imbalance.

**Ask yourself:**

Where is inclusion being built on personal sacrifice rather than shared responsibility?

 **Leadership Behavior Adjustment: Distribute Responsibility Intentionally**

Leaders must move beyond relying on informal champions to carry out institutional inclusion work. Sustainable leadership requires intentionally spreading responsibility across roles, departments, and leadership teams.

Leaders model this shift when they:

- Assign inclusion responsibilities formally rather than informally
- Protect time and capacity for those leading equity-related work
- Rotate leadership roles instead of relying on the same individuals
- Recognize inclusion labor as a legitimate professional contribution

When responsibility is shared, inclusion becomes institutional rather than personal.

 **Structural or Cultural Reinforcement: Build Systems That Support Inclusive Practice**

Inclusion becomes sustainable only when embedded in organizational systems. Without structural support, even the most committed staff eventually disengage.

Identify one system-level adjustment that strengthens inclusive practice, such as:

- Integrating inclusion goals into performance and planning structures
- Providing institutional resources for diversity and belonging initiatives
- Creating cross-functional inclusion teams
- Establishing clear accountability for inclusive outcomes

When inclusion is structurally supported, progress no longer depends on individual endurance.

---

## Leadership Anchor: Build Inclusion That Does Not Require Sacrifice

True inclusion does not ask a few people to carry the emotional weight for everyone else. Sustainable leaders design systems in which belonging is created collectively and responsibility is shared equitably. When inclusion is built through structure rather than sacrifice, organizations become stronger, more resilient, and more just.

## Partnership as Leadership Architecture 

Tokenized leadership weakens both culture and capacity. Invisible labor quietly drains energy, even when intentions are genuine. Partnership shifts representation into shared responsibility instead of isolated expectations. Inclusion stabilizes when contribution becomes a collective effort rather than an individual one.

## Part III Synthesis

### From Individual Leadership to Collective Culture

If Part II strengthened the leader's internal posture, Part III has widened the frame.

This section shifts the leadership perspective outward — from individual emotional steadiness to cultural responsibility within the system. Through generational dynamics, community involvement, equity navigation, inclusive team design, and relational bridge-building, a key truth has emerged: leadership is no longer just a solitary act of competence. Instead, it is a cultural process influenced by how responsibility, voice, and authority are shared.

Modern educational leaders do more than just manage instruction, staff performance, or policy. They navigate identity, history, power, belonging, and difference — often within the same conversation. They interpret generational expectations, respond to community stories, lead equity efforts, and maintain coherence in environments where cultural realities overlap and sometimes clash.

These chapters make one thing clear: culture doesn't change through intention alone. It changes through structure. It is shaped by repeated actions, reinforced by decision-making pathways, and shown in responsibility patterns. Culture isn't what leaders state; it's what systems consistently reward, protect, or overlook.

When generational tension is viewed as contextual rather than personal, collaboration replaces suspicion. When community identity is valued instead of being dismissed, trust deepens. When cultural flexibility becomes disciplined practice rather than occasional adjustment, alignment grows stronger. When equity work is grounded in steadiness instead of urgency or polarization, institutions can remain intact while they evolve. When inclusion is structurally distributed rather than emotionally concentrated, sustainability becomes achievable.

Together, these shifts redefine what leadership culture truly is.

Culture is not rhetoric.

It is reinforcement.

It is the normalization of certain behaviors over others.

It is the pattern of who carries what — and who does not.

Part III also reveals a sobering leadership insight: equity, inclusion, and cultural responsiveness cannot rely solely on goodwill. When emotional labor is concentrated among a few voices, fatigue deepens and fragmentation occurs. When the responsibility for cultural navigation is placed on individual leaders rather than integrated systems, progress becomes fragile. Without partnerships embedded in design, cultural work becomes inconsistent, costly, and prone to backlash.

This section has therefore invited leaders to examine not only what they believe, but how their institutions function.

To observe where labor is hidden, where responsibility is centered, where voice is undervalued, and where belonging depends more on personal stamina than institutional structure.

Awareness, however, is only the midpoint of transformation.

Emotional integrity stabilizes leaders. Cultural flexibility stabilizes relationships. But neither maintains longevity unless identity and design evolve with them.

Part IV advances the conversation into a higher level. It examines how leaders adapt without losing themselves, how identity changes without disappearing, and how authority grows without becoming isolating. It questions how leadership can be both practically responsive now and structurally strong over time.

Part III expanded leadership responsibility beyond the individual.

Part IV emphasizes leadership continuity — ensuring that cultural awareness becomes a lasting framework rather than a fleeting alignment.

From awareness of difference
to design that endures.

# PART IV

## IDENTITY AGILITY ACROSS EDUCATIONAL LEADERSHIP

### Academic Identity and Leadership Transition

In higher education, leadership often requires a profound identity shift long before it requires new technical skills. Scholars become administrators. Faculty peers become supervisors. Disciplinary experts become institutional decision-makers. The transition is rarely procedural; it is existential.

Many postsecondary leaders experience a quiet disorientation as they move from intellectual authority within a field to relational authority within an organization. The metrics change. The expectations expand. The relational dynamics shift. What once defined professional identity—research, teaching, scholarly contribution—must now coexist with governance, enrollment pressures, accreditation cycles, budget decisions, and personnel leadership.

Without intentional identity integration, these transitions can produce disconnection, role confusion, and professional loneliness. Leaders may feel suspended between identities—no longer fully faculty, not yet fully administrator. Collegial relationships recalibrate.

Peer networks thin. The intellectual clarity that once grounded their work may feel replaced by political navigation.

Identity agility in university systems protects intellectual integrity while expanding leadership capacity. It enables leaders to grow into broader responsibility without abandoning the core values and professional commitments that first shaped their vocation. It allows the scholar to remain intact while the administrator emerges.

The principles explored in this section apply directly to faculty-to-chair transitions, dean and provost leadership pathways, and any academic role that requires influence without micromanagement. Identity agility safeguards coherence in environments where authority shifts faster than identity stabilizes.

## Identity Agility for Educational Leaders

If emotional integrity anchors leaders internally and cultural flexibility shapes how they navigate relational difference, identity agility determines whether they can grow without losing themselves.

Educational leadership today no longer offers stable boundaries. Expectations evolve faster than titles. Responsibilities expand without proportional authority. Leaders are asked to serve simultaneously as instructional experts, emotional regulators, cultural interpreters, equity advocates, crisis managers, and institutional representatives. In many cases, these expectations coexist within a single role.

In this climate, leadership is not defined solely by what leaders do. It is defined by who they must become—and how often they must recalibrate that becoming.

Part IV centers identity agility as a leadership discipline. It examines what happens when leaders are required to embody roles that stretch, challenge, or even contradict earlier versions of themselves. It explores the emotional and psychological cost of continual adaptation without adequate integration.

## Leadership Identity Under Pressure

Leadership identity develops gradually through experience, mentorship, and meaning-making. It is shaped by professional calling, personal values, formative successes, and early models of authority. Over time, leaders construct an internal narrative of who they are and how they lead.

When institutional demands evolve faster than identity can integrate them, strain emerges. Leaders may feel tension between competing expectations or experience quiet dissonance between their values and their role requirements. This strain is often mislabeled as burnout or disengagement. More accurately, it reflects identity overload—the accumulation of responsibility without space for reflection or recalibration.

Identity overload does not indicate weakness. It signals that adaptation has outpaced integration.

## The Cost of Role Compression

As leadership responsibilities multiply, boundaries often contract. Leaders are expected to embody composure while managing uncertainty, to demonstrate confidence while navigating ambiguity, and to hold institutional values even when personal questions remain unresolved.

Over time, this compression can diminish clarity. Leaders may quietly ask themselves what parts of their identity remain permissible within their role and what must remain concealed. They may struggle to reconcile past versions of themselves with present expectations.

Part IV approaches these questions not as private crises but as predictable leadership dynamics within complex systems. Identity strain is not a personal flaw. It is a structural consequence of expanding responsibility without distributed support.

## Adapting Without Disappearing

Identity agility is not about constant reinvention or emotional shapeshifting. It is coherence amid change. It is the ability to expand without dissolving, to adapt without abandoning core values, and to grow without sacrificing stability for authenticity.

Agile leaders think carefully. They recognize when past stories no longer help with their current duties. They choose integration over separation. They adapt to changing situations without losing control of their leadership narrative.

This section explores how leaders can stay flexible without losing focus, be responsive without acting impulsively, and remain adaptive without sacrificing clarity about their identity.

## Identity as a Leadership Resource

Instead of viewing identity as something to control or diminish, Part IV presents identity as a key strategic leadership asset. When used intentionally, identity enhances relational trust, decision-making consistency, and long-term sustainability.

Leaders who cultivate identity agility are better equipped to guide others through role transitions, professional uncertainty, and identity-related stress. They model growth without collapse and stability without rigidity.

Identity becomes not a liability under pressure, but a resource for navigating it.

## Preparing for the Next Stage of Leadership

The chapters that follow explore identity from multiple vantage points: personal growth under pressure, teacher identity and professional loneliness, role transitions and promotion, and the reflective work required when students or staff mirror unresolved tensions back to leadership.

This work is not introspection for its own sake. It is preparation for durability.

Educational leadership in this era demands more than endurance. It requires leaders capable of adapting without fragmentation, holding complexity without confusion, and evolving alongside their institutions without erasing themselves.

Identity agility makes that endurance sustainable.

Without it, even emotionally intelligent and culturally responsive leadership eventually reaches its limit.

## Evolving Without Erosion

Leadership identity is not fixed. It evolves through cycles of transition, discomfort, promotion, criticism, loss, and growth. It is shaped not only by authority earned but by expectations absorbed and systems navigated under ongoing pressure.

Identity agility is the ability to adapt without losing integrity—to grow without sacrificing coherence. It helps leaders maintain authority without control and show vulnerability without losing stability. In environments marked by change and unpredictability, identity agility supports adaptation while keeping internal stability.

Yet identity strain intensifies when evolution happens in isolation. When expectations grow without structural adjustments, leadership identity can gradually turn into performance. Leaders project stability while privately managing fragmentation. When transitions lack institutional support, professional loneliness deepens—even in visible authority.

Partnership guards identity from deterioration by redistributing expectations before they become a silent burden. It makes growth a collective effort rather than a private deal. Leadership identity grows stronger when transitions are supported, authority shifts are organized, and stewardship is shared.

Leadership that continually reinvents itself alone eventually fractures. Leadership supported through shared design matures.

Identity agility is personal work. Its durability depends on collective architecture.

## Partnership Lens

Identity evolves, but it should not erode under isolated pressure. What appears as burnout is often concentrated expectation. Leadership coherence strengthens when structural support expands alongside responsibility. Agility endures when leaders are supported through shared stewardship rather than solitary adaptation.

# CHAPTER 14

## YOUR IDENTITY AS A LEADER IN A SHIFTING PROFESSION

### Global Leadership Spotlight

#### Country Focus: United Arab Emirates
#### Leadership Identity in Rapid Reform

The United Arab Emirates has rapidly and steadily modernized its education system by investing in international curricula, digital learning infrastructure, teacher development, and national education reform initiatives. Schools across the country often operate using hybrid models that combine global educational frameworks with national values, language priorities, and cultural identity goals. As a result, educational leaders often work in environments marked by ongoing policy changes and institutional transformations.

In rapidly changing environments, leadership roles seldom remain the same. Leaders are required to adjust to new accountability systems, multicultural staff teams, diverse student groups, and shifting national education priorities. This rate of change demands more than just technical skills—it calls for identity flexibility. Leaders must constantly reexamine how they see themselves professionally, balancing global best practices with local cultural responsibilities and institutional expectations.

The UAE's experience underscores a broader leadership truth: when systems change rapidly, leadership identity must also evolve. Leaders who resist adapting their identity often face internal conflict and role-related stress. Those who cultivate flexibility in how they interpret authority, influence, and professional purpose are better equipped to lead through change without losing clarity. Being adaptable in identity helps leaders stay grounded while managing complexity.

**Leadership Reflection:**

How is your leadership identity evolving in response to system change, and what beliefs or habits may need to shift to support that growth?

Leadership identity must evolve without dissolving.

Few leaders enter education expecting their roles to change beneath them. Most are ready to develop in their skills, responsibilities, and influence. Far fewer are prepared for the quieter challenge of modern leadership: the need to continuously renegotiate who they are as professionals while the profession itself is being redefined.

In today's educational landscape, leadership identity is not stable over time. It is constantly tested, stretched, and reshaped by changing expectations, expanding roles, and different ideas of success. Leaders are asked to adapt nonstop, often without the language to describe what they are losing in the process.

This chapter encourages leaders to see leadership identity not as something to defend at all costs, nor as something to give up for relevance, but as a dynamic framework—one that can grow with integrity rather than fall apart under pressure.

## When the Role Changes Faster Than the Self

Educational leadership once followed mostly predictable paths. Experience gained authority. Tenure provided clarity. Institutional norms gave stability. Although leadership was never truly static, it was consistent enough for identity to stabilize.

That coherence has eroded.

Leaders today are asked to respond to crises that previously didn't define their role, manage emotional and cultural work that was once considered peripheral, and take on accountability without having proportional control. Expectations grow faster than meaning can be understood.

When roles change faster than leaders can adapt, identity strain appears. Leaders may feel capable but disconnected, accomplished yet uneasy. They might observe a growing gap between how they lead and why they initially chose to lead.

This is not failure. It is a sign that identity hasn't been given enough time or structure to develop alongside responsibility.

## Who You Are Becoming

Leadership identity is not only shaped by what leaders do, but by what they repeatedly practice under pressure. Over time, leaders become what the role rewards.

For some, this means becoming more guarded, more transactional, or more emotionally reserved than they initially intended. For others, it involves becoming hyper-responsible—overfunctioning in ways that seem necessary but aren't sustainable. Still, some find themselves shrinking their leadership presence to avoid conflict, scrutiny, or exhaustion.

These shifts often happen gradually. Leaders rarely wake up and choose to abandon their values. Instead, they adapt to survive. The risk isn't in adapting itself, but in doing so without awareness.

Reflecting on who you are becoming is not self-indulgent; it is a duty of professional responsibility. Leaders who remain unaware of their identity drift risk waking up one day to find themselves effective but unrecognizable to themselves.

## What Must Be Released

Identity agility demands both letting go and gaining.

Many leaders hold outdated beliefs about what effective leadership is—beliefs shaped by earlier phases of the profession or by mentors whose context no longer fits. These beliefs often include unspoken expectations of self-sacrifice, emotional invisibility, or constant availability.

Holding onto these expectations in a changed landscape creates dissonance. Leaders feel they are failing at standards that no longer serve the role—or the people within it.

Release does not mean abandoning excellence. It means letting go of leadership myths that equate endurance with effectiveness, silence with strength, or self-erasure with service.

Leaders also need to let go of roles they have outgrown. As responsibilities grow, holding onto every task becomes both impossible and unnecessary. Giving up control isn't a loss of authority; it's a recalibration of purpose.

What leaders release shapes what becomes possible next.

## The Fear Beneath Identity Change

Identity change often causes fear—not because leaders oppose growth, but because identity provides meaning. When leadership identity evolves, leaders may fear losing credibility, a sense of belonging, or clarity.

Questions come up quietly. If I lead differently, will I still earn respect? If I set boundaries, will I still be effective? If I admit uncertainty, will I still be trusted?

These fears are seldom discussed openly in professional settings. Yet, they deeply influence leadership behavior. Leaders might stick to familiar patterns not because they are effective, but because they feel more secure.

Identity agility doesn't eliminate fear; it helps leaders move forward without letting fear control every decision.

## Leading Without Losing Yourself

Leading without losing yourself doesn't mean staying the same. It means staying true to who you are.

A coherent leadership identity aligns values, behavior, and boundaries—even as strategies evolve. It enables leaders to adapt their expression without abandoning core commitments. It creates space for growth without causing fragmentation.

Leaders who maintain coherence are better able to:

- Make decisions without excessive self-doubt
- Navigate conflict without personalizing it
- Set boundaries without guilt
- Remain emotionally present without overidentifying

This coherence is not achieved through certainty. It is achieved through reflection and intentional choice.

## Identity as an Ongoing Practice

Leadership identity isn't something leaders define once and keep the same. It needs to be revisited during transition points—such as role changes, policy shifts, organizational crises, or personal milestones.

Identity agility means taking time to ask reflective questions. Which parts of my leadership still match my values? Which parts seem performative or defensive instead of genuine? What am I holding onto out of habit rather than purpose?

These questions are not distractions from leadership work. They are central to it.

Leaders who neglect identity work often compensate with control, overwork, or emotional withdrawal. Leaders who engage it intentionally achieve clarity and sustainability.

## The Gift of Conscious Evolution

There is no going back to a simpler form of educational leadership. The profession has transformed, and leaders must adapt accordingly. The question isn't whether identity will change, but how it will.

Unconscious evolution leads to erosion. Conscious evolution leads to integration.

This chapter encourages leaders to see identity change as a disciplined practice rather than a personal crisis. To understand that releasing outdated narratives is not a loss but a form of alignment. And to realize that leadership integrity isn't about remaining the same but about staying whole.

The upcoming chapters will expand on this work—exploring teacher identity, professional loneliness, role transitions, and the reflective mirror that students often offer.

But that work begins here.

Leadership identity must evolve.

It does not have to dissolve.

When leaders allow themselves to grow with awareness, they do more than just survive a changing profession. They demonstrate what sustainable leadership looks like—steady, adaptable, and rooted in self-knowledge rather than self-sacrifice.

# INSIDE THE CLASSROOM

## When Leadership No Longer Feels Familiar

The principal stood at the front of the auditorium during a school assembly, scanning the room full of students and staff. They had delivered this same speech countless times over the years. The words were practiced. The structure is familiar. And yet, something felt different.

Later that day, sitting alone in their office, they reflected on the shift. The profession had changed. The expectations had changed. And quietly, they had changed too.

They were no longer the same leader who stepped into the role years ago, full of confidence, energy, and a clear sense of identity. Now, leadership demanded more emotional understanding, increased public scrutiny, and greater complexity. It felt less like assuming a role and more like constantly redefining who they were becoming.

Leadership identity is not fixed. It changes under pressure. Those who resist this change often face frustration and stagnation. Those who allow their identity to adapt — while holding onto core values — find new ways to stay steady.

## LEADERSHIP NEXT STEPS — Leadership Identity in Rapid Reform

### Awareness Shift: Recognize Identity Strain as a Leadership Signal

Rapid reform environments place continuous pressure on leadership identity. New policies, evolving expectations, and shifting accountability structures often require leaders to adapt quickly without sufficient time to integrate change meaningfully. Over time, this can create identity strain — a sense of misalignment between personal leadership values and professional role demands.

Begin noticing moments when leadership feels performative rather than authentic, or when decisions feel disconnected from your core purpose. These signals are not personal shortcomings. They are indicators that identity recalibration is needed.

**Ask yourself:**

Where has rapid change pulled me away from my core leadership values?

 **Leadership Behavior Adjustment: Lead From Anchored Values**

Sustainable leadership in reform-heavy environments requires a strong internal anchor. Leaders who remain grounded in clearly articulated values are better able to navigate external change without becoming reactive or fragmented.

Leaders practice anchored leadership when they:

- Clarify non-negotiable leadership principles
- Align daily decisions with long-term purpose
- Communicate values consistently during periods of change
- Resist pressure to compromise integrity for short-term approval

When leaders lead from values rather than volatility, credibility and trust increase.

 **Structural or Cultural Reinforcement: Build Identity-Sustaining Leadership Systems**

Leadership identity cannot be sustained through personal discipline alone. Institutions must create structures that support reflection, continuity, and professional coherence. Without this support, leaders are forced to recalibrate in isolation.

Identify one structural practice that supports leadership identity sustainability, such as:

- Creating leadership reflection and mentoring spaces
- Establishing continuity frameworks during reform cycles
- Protecting time for strategic leadership planning
- Supporting peer networks across reform environments

When identity is structurally supported, leaders are more likely to remain grounded despite ongoing change.

## Leadership Anchor: Lead Change Without Losing Yourself

Rapid reform does not require leaders to abandon their identity in order to remain effective. Sustainable leadership emerges when leaders adapt externally while remaining internally anchored. When leaders hold clarity of purpose amid shifting systems, they create stability not only for themselves, but for the communities they serve.

## Partnership as Leadership Architecture

Leadership identity develops through pressure, promotion, and change. Growth without structural support turns expansion into performance issues. Partnership aligns expectations through intentional planning, allowing identity to grow without splitting. Agility remains when responsibility increases alongside authority.

# CHAPTER 15

## TEACHER IDENTITY, ROLE FATIGUE, AND PROFESSIONAL LONELINESS

### Global Leadership Spotlight

#### Country Focus: South Korea
#### Teacher Identity and Professional Pressure

South Korea's education system is globally recognized for high academic achievement and strong student performance. The country's focus on standardized testing, competitive university admission, and strict academic standards has created a performance-oriented school environment. In this setting, teachers are often expected to deliver high-quality instruction while managing heavy workloads and societal pressures.

Despite these outcomes, education researchers and workforce organizations have noted ongoing issues related to educator stress, professional isolation, and emotional fatigue. Teachers often report long hours, pressure to meet performance standards, and limited opportunities for emotional processing within the professional culture. While achievement metrics remain strong, maintaining emotional sustainability in the workforce remains a leadership challenge.

South Korea's experience highlights a key leadership lesson: performance metrics often overlook the true cost of success. When achievement is valued without simultaneous investment in emotional well-being, professional identity becomes closely linked to output rather than purpose. Effective leadership depends on systems that safeguard human capacity along with academic excellence.

**Leadership Reflection:**

How does your organization intentionally support emotional well-being while maintaining high performance expectations?

Teachers are often surrounded—yet alone.

Schools are busy places. Hallways are crowded. Meetings happen constantly. Collaboration is encouraged. Yet, many teachers feel a deep sense of professional loneliness that is rarely acknowledged, rarely addressed, and often misunderstood.

This loneliness does not stem from a lack of people. Instead, it arises from role overload, fragmented identity, and the silent expectation to stay strong no matter what. Teachers are asked to juggle multiple roles—educator, caregiver, disciplinarian, advocate, data analyst, crisis responder—often without enough support or acknowledgment of the emotional challenges involved.

This chapter explores how these pressures influence teacher identity and lead to fatigue that extends well beyond workload.

## Role Overload as Identity Strain

Teaching has always called for flexibility. What has changed is the number of roles teachers are expected to assume simultaneously—and how quickly they must switch between them.

A teacher may shift from delivering rigorous instruction to managing student trauma, from collaborating with colleagues to communicating with families, from meeting accountability measures to supporting social-emotional needs—all within the same day. Each role has its own emotional demands, norms, and expectations.

When these roles accumulate without proper integration, teachers experience role overload. Over time, this overload leads to identity strain. Teachers start to feel stretched thin not only in terms of time but also in their sense of self. They may struggle to clearly define who they are within the profession because the role no longer feels unified or coherent.

This fragmentation is exhausting precisely because it requires constant emotional recalibration.

## Identity Fragmentation in Plain Sight

Identity fragmentation happens when teachers have to compartmentalize parts of themselves to handle conflicting demands. Professional expectations might demand emotional neutrality, while students need emotional engagement. Institutional metrics may prioritize efficiency, but meaningful teaching requires relational depth.

Teachers learn to handle these contradictions quietly. They adapt, perform, and follow rules. From the outside, they seem capable and calm. Inside, however, they might feel more disconnected from the values and motives that drew them to the profession.

Fragmentation is rarely recognized because teachers continue to function. They meet expectations. They support others. They hold things together.

But functioning is not the same as belonging.

## The Loneliness of Being "the Strong One"

One of the most isolating dynamics in teaching is the unspoken expectation to be strong.

Reliable, emotionally steady, and competent teachers often become the ones others depend on. They are trusted with extra responsibilities, challenging students, informal mentoring, and emotional support for colleagues. Their strength leads others to ask for more.

Over time, these teachers may find themselves carrying invisible labor without reciprocal care. They are seen as capable, not as human. They may hesitate to express fatigue or doubt for fear of disappointing others or being perceived as less reliable.

This creates a particular kind of loneliness—the loneliness of being needed but not supported, of being surrounded by people yet lacking space to be fully seen.

## Professional Loneliness as a Leadership Issue

Teacher loneliness is often viewed as a personal issue rather than a leadership problem. However, it stems from structural factors: how roles are structured, how duties are allocated, and how emotional expression is managed within the institution.

When schools reward endurance without providing recovery, loneliness increases. When collaboration emphasizes output over connection, teachers feel replaceable rather than appreciated. When vulnerability is discouraged, teachers withdraw inward.

Leadership plays a vital role in whether professional loneliness is reinforced or eased. Leaders who see loneliness as a systemic problem can intervene thoughtfully—by redistributing work, creating safe spaces for reflection, and demonstrating relational care without overexposure.

## The Cost of Ignoring Teacher Identity

When teacher identity strain is left unaddressed, predictable consequences ensue. Engagement drops. Creativity shrinks. Retention declines. Teachers may stay in the profession physically but disconnect emotionally, doing what is required while withholding what once made their teaching meaningful.

This withdrawal is often unnoticed until it becomes widespread. By the time turnover increases or morale drops visibly, identity erosion has been happening for years.

Addressing teacher identity isn't about individual counseling or resilience training. It's about restoring coherence—helping teachers unify their roles rather than feel fractured under them.

## Creating Space for Identity Integration

Leaders can foster identity integration by recognizing teachers as whole professionals instead of just sets of tasks. This includes acknowledging the emotional complexity of the role, legitimizing the need for boundaries, and establishing structures that enable teachers to reflect, connect, and recalibrate.

This does not require leaders to solve every problem teachers encounter. It asks them to recognize the problem clearly and respond purposefully rather than based on assumptions.

When teachers feel recognized as whole individuals, loneliness lessens. When identity is permitted to integrate rather than fragment, fatigue becomes manageable rather than destructive.

## From Isolation to Connection

This chapter does not suggest that teaching can ever be free of stress. Instead, it emphasizes that stress does not have to lead to isolation. Teachers flourish in environments where strength is not mistaken for unlimited capacity, where contribution does not require self-sacrifice, and where professionalism includes the right to be human. When these conditions are present, educators are not just surviving the demands of their roles—they are supported in maintaining their purpose and presence.

The upcoming chapters will continue this exploration by examining role transitions, promotions, departures, and the reflective work leaders must undertake to support others through change. However, that work begins with acknowledgment. Teachers often feel surrounded but isolated. Lasting leadership learns to bridge that gap. By addressing role fatigue, identity fragmentation, and professional loneliness as systemic issues rather than personal flaws, leaders create schools where teachers do more than just survive—they belong.

# INSIDE THE CLASSROOM

## Surrounded, Yet Alone

The teacher sat in a crowded staff room, scrolling through lesson plans while colleagues chatted nearby. Laughter filled the space. Conversations overlapped. On the surface, it felt communal.

Inside, they felt disconnected.

They had become the one others relied on — the steady presence, the dependable problem-solver, the person who rarely asked for help. Over time, strength had turned into isolation. Vulnerability felt risky. Silence felt safer.

Later that week, during a rare honest moment with a colleague, they admitted feeling lonely in the role. The relief was instant. Not because the problem vanished, but because it was finally shared.

Professional loneliness often masks itself as competence. Identity agility demands that leaders and educators create room for genuine connection—not merely functional collaboration.

---

## LEADERSHIP NEXT STEPS —
## Teacher Identity and Professional Pressure

**Awareness Shift: Recognize Professional Loneliness as a Leadership Risk**

Teacher identity strain is not only about workload. It is often rooted in isolation, emotional invisibility, and the quiet erosion of professional belonging. When educators feel unseen, unsupported, or disconnected from purpose, role fatigue intensifies and commitment weakens.

Begin noticing where teachers appear emotionally withdrawn, disengaged, or overly self-reliant. These are not signs of apathy. They are indicators that professional connection and identity support are missing.

**Ask yourself:**
Where are teachers carrying emotional and professional weight alone instead of collectively?

### 2  Leadership Behavior Adjustment: Rebuild Professional Connection

Leaders play a central role in shaping whether educators experience their work as isolated labor or shared purpose. Intentional leadership presence can interrupt professional loneliness by restoring relational connection and identity affirmation.

Leaders strengthen connections when they:

- Regularly acknowledge professional contributions beyond performance metrics
- Create space for reflective dialogue about purpose and growth
- Listen for emotional subtext, not just instructional outcomes
- Encourage collaboration without turning it into additional workload

When leaders invest in relational leadership, teachers are more likely to remain engaged and professionally anchored.

### 3  Structural or Cultural Reinforcement: Design Identity-Sustaining Work Environments

Professional belonging cannot depend solely on individual relationships. Institutions must create systems that support identity continuity and emotional sustainability. Without structural reinforcement, the connection remains fragile and inconsistent.

Identify one system-level adjustment that supports teacher identity sustainability, such as:

- Building mentorship and peer-support structures
- Protecting collaborative planning and reflection time

- Reducing role overload through clearer responsibility boundaries
- Creating leadership pathways that honor professional growth

When identity support is built into organizational design, teachers are less likely to experience chronic role fatigue and isolation.

---

## "
## Leadership Anchor: Protect Professional Identity to Sustain the Profession

Teachers cannot be expected to carry professional purpose in isolation. Sustainable leadership recognizes that identity support is not optional — it is foundational to retention, morale, and long-term educational stability. When leaders intentionally protect professional identity, they strengthen not only individual educators but the future of the profession itself.

## Partnership as Leadership Architecture

Visibility does not eliminate isolation. Role expansion without relational reinforcement increases fatigue and quiet loneliness. Partnership normalizes shared adjustment during professional transitions. Identity coherence strengthens when leaders are not left to evolve alone.

# CHAPTER 16
## SUPPORTING STAFF THROUGH ROLE CHANGES, PROMOTIONS, AND DEPARTURES

### Global Leadership Spotlight

#### Country Focus: Rwanda
#### Leadership Transitions and System Building

Rwanda has consistently invested in rebuilding and strengthening its education system as part of broader national development efforts. Leadership development has been identified as a vital part of this process, with initiatives focused on training school leaders, enhancing institutional capacity, and improving governance structures. In this context, leadership transitions are increasingly seen not just as routine administrative changes but as strategic opportunities to reinforce system stability and long-term vision.

As schools and districts undergo leadership changes, new leaders are often tasked with maintaining continuity while advancing reform priorities. These transitions need careful planning, clear communication, and strong support to keep institutional memory and protect the organizational culture. When leadership changes are rushed or lack proper backing, instability tends to grow. When transitions are regarded as structured moments of identity, institutions are better able to maintain progress.

Rwanda's experience highlights a key leadership principle: transitions shape organizational identity. How leaders join, leave, and transfer responsibilities impacts trust, morale, and cohesion. Effective leadership systems emphasize succession planning, mentorship, and transition support to ensure stability instead of disruption.

**Leadership Reflection:**

How does your organization prepare for leadership transitions, and what systems are in place to protect continuity, culture, and institutional memory?

Transitions carry emotional weight long after logistics are handled.

In schools and educational institutions, role changes are often viewed as administrative events. A promotion is announced. A resignation is processed. A role change is communicated. Schedules are adjusted, responsibilities are realigned, and the system moves forward. From an operational perspective, the transition is considered complete.

From a human perspective, it is often just beginning.

This chapter redefines promotions, departures, and role changes not just as staffing decisions but as moments of identity—moments when professional self-understanding is disrupted, renegotiated, or reshaped. When leaders overlook this emotional aspect, transitions can have lasting effects on morale, trust, and long-term stability.

## The Emotional Undercurrent of Professional Transition

Every role carries identity. It shapes how individuals see themselves, how others relate to them, and how meaning is constructed within the institution. When a role changes, identity does not automatically update.

A teacher promoted to leadership may feel pride along with a sense of loss—losing their peer identity, classroom connection, or the clarity that came with a familiar role. A staff member changing responsibilities might experience relief mixed with uncertainty about their sense of belonging or their competence. When a colleague leaves, it can trigger grief, resentment, or fear, even if the departure is voluntary and positive.

These emotional responses are seldom acknowledged in public. Institutions usually focus on gratitude, excitement, or continuity, leaving little space for the more complex feelings people experience privately.

When emotional undercurrents are ignored, they do not disappear. They surface later as disengagement, resistance, or relational strain.

## Promotions as Identity Disruption

Promotion is often assumed to be purely affirming. In reality, it can be destabilizing.

New leaders often face internal conflict between who they used to be and who they are expected to become. Relationships change. Boundaries become stricter. Sources of reassurance shift. People may feel pressured to prove their legitimacy while still grieving the loss of their former identity.

When leaders believe that a promotion equates to confidence, they overlook the opportunity to support identity integration. New leaders might quietly struggle, unsure whether uncertainty indicates inadequacy or simply a normal transition.

Effective leadership sees promotion as a developmental milestone. It needs room for reflection, mentorship that nurtures both identity and skills, and the freedom to grow into authority without feeling the need to demonstrate certainty prematurely.

## Role Shifts and Invisible Loss

Not all transitions involve upward movement. Lateral shifts, role redesigns, or reassignments often come with unseen costs.

A teacher who leaves a role they loved might feel diminished, even if the change was necessary or asked for. A staff member whose duties change could question their value or future at the institution. These feelings are often minimized because they don't fit the celebratory stories.

Leaders who overlook these moments unintentionally send the message that emotional impact is less important than organizational needs. Over time, this damages trust and reinforces the idea that people are replaceable.

Acknowledging loss does not undermine professionalism. It honors reality.

## Departures as Collective Experience

Staff departures are often seen as individual choices. While that may be true, departures are also collective events. They impact team identity, workload, and emotional climate.

When departures are announced only through logistical updates, colleagues are left to process their feelings privately. This can lead to unresolved grief, speculation, or resentment—especially when departures occur frequently or go unexplained.

Leaders who recognize the emotional aspect of departure promote healthier closure. Highlighting contributions, providing space for reactions, and discussing what will change—and what will stay the same—help teams process loss without losing stability.

Avoidance, by contrast, leaves unanswered questions that undermine trust.

## Leadership Presence During Transition

Leadership presence matters most during transitions—not because leaders must have answers, but because their stance signals whether people matter beyond function.

Presence during transition means staying involved even after the announcement. It includes checking in, listening patiently without rushing to solve issues, and accepting discomfort without avoiding it. It also requires consistency—making sure promises made during the transition are kept afterward.

Leaders who disappear after a change is implemented show that they view transition as a task rather than a relational process. Leaders who stay engaged demonstrate reliability.

## Identity Agility in Others

Supporting staff through transitions requires leaders to recognize identity agility not only in themselves, but in others.

People adapt to change at different speeds. Some adjust quickly, while others need time to rebuild their meaning and confidence. Leaders who expect everyone to respond the same way unintentionally create pressure to modify behavior rather than support genuine experience.

This does not mean delaying progress indefinitely. It means allowing space for integration while maintaining direction.

When leaders normalize the emotional complexity of transitions, staff are less likely to internalize their struggles as failure.

## The Cost of Mishandled Transitions

When transitions are mishandled, the impact goes beyond the individual. Teams become more cautious. Trust diminishes. Staff might hesitate to pursue growth opportunities if they think the 'identity cost' will be ignored. Others may emotionally disengage to shield themselves from future disruptions.

Over time, institutions build a reputation—sometimes unspoken—as places where people are moved along rather than truly supported. This reputation influences retention, leadership pipelines, and organizational culture.

## Leading Transitions with Integrity

This chapter does not suggest that leaders can eliminate the emotional impact of change. Instead, it affirms that leaders can manage it responsibly. Leading transitions with integrity means understanding that identity does not change instantly. It involves recognizing loss alongside opportunity, uncertainty alongside progress, and emotion alongside efficiency. When leaders focus on the human side of transition, they strengthen the system rather than weaken it.

Promotions, role shifts, and departures are more than just staffing changes. There are moments when identity is redefined. Lasting leadership recognizes this truth and responds not only with plans and timelines but also with presence, clarity, and compassion. The next chapter will once again turn inward, exploring how leaders are shaped by those they serve—and how students, staff, and systems reflect unresolved identity work. Because leadership is not solely about guiding others through change, it is about understanding how change influences all of us, whether we acknowledge it or not.

# INSIDE THE CLASSROOM

## The Goodbye That Was Harder Than Expected

When the teacher announced they were leaving, the team responded with congratulations and best wishes. The promotion was well earned. The transition was smooth. Still, the staff felt the change right away. The classroom sat empty for days before a replacement arrived. Students asked questions. Colleagues noticed the absence. The emotional impact of the change lingered well after the logistical adjustments were finished.

For the departing teacher, the change brought excitement mixed with quiet grief. They were leaving behind a familiar identity—a role that had shaped their daily rhythm and sense of belonging. Leadership transitions are not just staffing moves. They are moments that define identity. How leaders manage these transitions determines whether people feel supported or simply replaced.

---

## LEADERSHIP NEXT STEPS — Leadership Transitions and System Building

 **Awareness Shift: Recognize Transitions as Cultural Turning Points**

Role changes, promotions, and departures do more than change staffing structures. They shape culture, shift influence, and impact morale and identity throughout the organization. When transitions are seen as administrative tasks rather than leadership moments, instability quietly grows.

Start viewing transitions as cultural milestones. Focus on emotional reactions, informal power changes, and uncertainty that usually come with change. These dynamics show where leadership presence and structure are most important.

**Ask yourself:**

Where are staff transitions being managed procedurally instead of led relationally and strategically?

 **Leadership Behavior Adjustment: Lead Transitions With Clarity and Care**

Effective transition leadership balances operational clarity with emotional awareness. Leaders must communicate expectations, timelines, and roles while also acknowledging the relational impact of change.

Leaders model strong transition leadership when they:

- Communicate openly about role changes and organizational direction
- Support individuals stepping into new responsibilities
- Acknowledge contributions of departing staff with respect
- Maintain consistency during periods of uncertainty

When leaders handle transitions with transparency and care, trust and stability are preserved.

### Structural or Cultural Reinforcement: Build Succession-Ready Systems

Organizations become fragile when continuity depends on specific individuals rather than institutional design. Sustainable leadership requires systems that prepare for change rather than react to it.

Identify one system-level adjustment that strengthens leadership continuity, such as:

- Developing internal leadership pipelines
- Documenting institutional knowledge and processes
- Creating mentorship structures for emerging leaders
- Establishing succession planning practices

When continuity is built into structure, organizations remain resilient despite personnel change.

> ## Leadership Anchor: Lead Change While Preserving Continuity
>
> Leadership transitions don't have to destabilize organizations. When leaders view change as a chance to strengthen systems rather than disrupt them, continuity can be maintained. Sustainable leadership retains institutional memory, safeguards relational trust, and enhances capacity for the future — even as people move in and out of roles.

## Partnership as Leadership Architecture

Transitions reshape identity, whether acknowledged or not. When change is individualized, strain deepens beneath professionalism. Partnership structures that accompany role shifts and institutional change become vital. Continuity strengthens when leadership evolution is shared rather than solitary.

# CHAPTER 17

## WHEN STUDENTS BECOME THE MIRROR: THE PERSONAL IDENTITY WORK OF LEADERS

### Global Leadership Spotlight

**Country Focus: Kenya**
**Student-Centered Accountability**

Kenya's education system has undergone significant reform with the introduction of competency-based curriculum frameworks aimed at emphasizing skills development, learner-centered instruction, and comprehensive student growth. These reforms shift accountability from exam results alone and encourage educators and school leaders to focus on critical thinking, communication, creativity, and practical application of learning.

As a result, leadership accountability increasingly involves responsiveness to students' experiences and voices. Leaders are expected to consider how policies, instructional practices, and school culture affect student engagement and growth. This calls for moving beyond traditional top-down leadership models toward approaches that actively seek feedback from students and communities.

Kenya's experience underscores a broader leadership insight: students are not just recipients of leadership decisions—they are mirrors that reflect leadership effectiveness. When leaders consider student behavior, engagement, and feedback, they gather valuable insights into organizational culture, teaching quality, and relational climate. Reflection based on student experience enhances leadership development and institutional responsiveness.

**Leadership Reflection:**

What patterns in student engagement, feedback, or behavior might be offering insight into the impact of your leadership approach?

Students often surface what leaders avoid in themselves.

In education, leaders dedicate much of their time to outward focus—on outcomes, behavior, performance, and systems. However, some of the most important leadership work happens inwardly, often unexpectedly, when interactions with students trigger strong emotional reactions that seem disproportionate to the moment itself.

A student's defiance, disengagement, apathy, or intensity can evoke frustration, urgency, or self-doubt in leaders, extending beyond professional concern. These moments are often dismissed as stress or attributed solely to student behavior. However, they are often reflections—showing unresolved identity tensions, unmet expectations, or values that leaders have learned to hide to function.

This chapter explores how students become catalysts for personal identity work in leaders, and how growth emerges not by avoiding discomfort, but by engaging it with honesty and discipline.

## Emotional Triggers as Information

Emotional triggers are often seen as liabilities in leadership. Leaders are expected to stay calm, neutral, and unaffected—especially when interacting with students. When a reaction occurs, leaders might feel embarrassed, defensive, or eager to hide it.

Yet emotional triggers are not evidence of weakness. They are information.

A trigger indicates that something meaningful has been activated—such as an expectation, belief, or unexamined assumption. It may relate to a leader's personal educational background, values, or internalized standards about effort, respect, or success.

When leaders overlook these signals, triggers recur. When leaders examine them thoughtfully, they gain insight not only into themselves but also into how they behave in their roles.

This doesn't mean leaders focus their emotions during student interactions. Instead, it means they reflect afterward, asking what the reaction revealed and why it mattered.

## Projection in Leadership Relationships

Projection happens when leaders unconsciously assign their own fears, frustrations, or unresolved experiences to others. In educational environments, students are especially vulnerable to projection because they are still developing their identity and often express emotions openly.

A leader who values discipline might react strongly to perceived disengagement. A leader who overcame adversity through compliance could struggle with students who question authority. A leader who takes pride in resilience may feel threatened by students who openly express vulnerability without apology.

These reactions are rarely about the student alone. They are about meaning.

Projection becomes problematic when leaders treat students as symbols instead of individuals—punishing what seems intolerable rather than addressing the real issues. This dynamic can damage trust and increase conflict, often without leaders understanding the reasons behind it.

Awareness interrupts projection. Leaders who pause to examine their reactions regain agency. They move from reflex to reflection, from judgment to understanding.

## Discomfort as a Developmental Signal

Discomfort is often framed as something to eliminate quickly in schools. Leaders intervene, redirect, or escalate to restore order. While structure is necessary, constant avoidance of discomfort limits growth—for both students and leaders.

For leaders, discomfort often signals a mismatch between identity and reality. It may indicate that a long-held belief no longer fits the current context, or that a leadership stance needs recalibration.

Growth does not occur despite discomfort. It occurs through it.

Leaders who allow themselves to sit briefly with discomfort—without acting on or suppressing it—create space for learning. They recognize when a reaction is driven by habit rather than principle, or when control is used to manage anxiety rather than foster growth.

This self-awareness strengthens leadership presence. It reduces reactivity and increases intentionality.

## The Leader's Inner Classroom

Every leader has an internal classroom built from their own student experiences. Past successes, failures, praise, shame, and expectations shape how leaders interpret student behavior today.

When students challenge authority, disengage, or resist norms, leaders may unconsciously relive earlier experiences—either their own struggles or their own compliance. These memories influence emotional responses long before logic takes over.

Engaging in identity work enables leaders to distinguish between their past and present selves. It helps them respond to the student in front of them instead of an outdated internal narrative.

This is not therapy. It is professional self-knowledge.

## Leading Without Reacting

One of the most significant outcomes of this inner work is the ability to lead without reacting.

Reactive leadership feels urgent, corrective, and emotionally charged. Reflective leadership feels grounded, measured, and intentional. The difference lies not in temperament, but in awareness.

Leaders who recognize their triggers are less likely to escalate unnecessarily. They choose responses aligned with values rather than impulses. They model emotional regulation not by suppression, but by discernment.

Students notice this difference. Trust grows when leaders are predictable, not because they are rigid, but because they are self-aware.

## Modeling Growth Through Self-Awareness

Students learn as much from who leaders are as from what they enforce. Leaders who demonstrate humility, reflection, and growth embody a kind of authority that is both strong and empathetic. This doesn't mean leaders have to share personal struggles or openly talk about internal processes. Instead, it involves leading with authenticity rather than defensiveness. When leaders do this consistently, they foster environments where growth becomes the norm—not just for students but for adults as well.

## The Courage to Look Inward

It takes courage to acknowledge that students can surface unresolved parts of leadership identity. It is easier to attribute difficulty solely to behavior or policy. Yet leaders who engage this work gain depth, clarity, and resilience.

They lead with less ego and greater presence. They respond intentionally instead of reflexively. They stay steadier under pressure because they aren't battling their inner selves.

This chapter does not imply that leaders are accountable for every emotional reaction they have. Instead, it states that leaders are responsible for how they handle those reactions.

Students will keep reflecting on what leaders have not yet explored. The question is whether leaders see those moments as sources of frustration or as chances to grow.

Identity agility is not only about adapting to systems.

It is about meeting oneself honestly in the work.

And when leaders are willing to do that, leadership becomes not just a role, but a practice—one that evolves with integrity, depth, and purpose.

## INSIDE THE CLASSROOM

### When Students Reflect More Than Content

During a class discussion, a student challenged the teacher directly. The question was not inappropriate — but it was honest, raw, and uncomfortable.

The teacher felt a familiar reaction rise: defensiveness. Instead, they paused. They listened. They recognized something deeper beneath the moment.

The student's question mirrored a tension the teacher had been avoiding in themselves — uncertainty about change, frustration with the system, fatigue with constant adaptation.

Later that evening, the teacher reflected on the exchange. Students often surface what educators carry silently. They reflect not only academic gaps but also emotional and identity tensions.

Growth does not always come from new strategies. Sometimes it comes from allowing discomfort to reveal where leadership and identity still need room to expand.

# LEADERSHIP NEXT STEPS — Student-Centered Accountability

**Awareness Shift: Recognize Student Feedback as Leadership Reflection**

Students often reflect the emotional tone, expectations, and relational climate set by leadership. Behavioral challenges, disengagement, or resistance are not just classroom problems — they often indicate larger system and leadership issues.

Begin viewing student responses as leadership data rather than isolated discipline problems. Pay attention to patterns in student behavior, participation, and emotional expression. These patterns offer insight into how leadership decisions are shaping learning environments.

**Ask yourself:**

What are students' behaviors revealing about the culture we have created?

**Leadership Behavior Adjustment: Practice Reflective Leadership Presence**

When leaders let student experiences shape their leadership practice, accountability becomes growth-oriented rather than defensive. Reflective leadership requires humility, openness to feedback, and a willingness to adjust behavior when impact doesn't match intention.

Leaders strengthen student-centered accountability when they:

- Seek student voice in school improvement conversations
- Reflect on how policies affect student experience
- Model accountability when leadership missteps occur
- Adjust practices based on lived classroom realities

When leaders remain open to reflection, credibility and trust increase across the school community.

### 3. Structural or Cultural Reinforcement: Embed Student Voice Into Leadership Systems

Student-centered accountability cannot depend on individual leaders alone. Institutions must build structures that consistently elevate student perspectives.

Identify one system-level practice that strengthens student voice, such as:

- Creating student advisory councils or leadership forums
- Integrating student feedback into policy review processes
- Establishing formal listening channels between students and administration
- Incorporating student experience data into leadership planning

When student voice is structurally supported, accountability becomes continuous rather than reactive.

## Leadership Anchor: Let Student Experience Refine Leadership Identity

Students often reflect leadership impact more honestly than performance metrics. Leaders who allow student experiences to shape their growth develop deeper self-awareness, stronger relational leadership, and greater professional integrity. When leaders remain open to this reflection, accountability becomes a pathway to maturity rather than a threat to authority.

# Partnership as Leadership Architecture

Discomfort shows areas for growth rather than leadership failure. Reflection alone often causes defensiveness or self-protection. Partnership transforms insight into collective learning. Leadership grows when self-examination becomes a shared process instead of a private burden.

## Part IV Synthesis

### Sustaining Leadership Identity in a Profession That Keeps Changing

If the earlier sections of this book clarified emotional weight and expanded cultural responsibility, Part IV has intentionally turned inward. Not for introspection alone, but toward the effort that enables longevity.

Educational leadership today operates within ongoing change. Reform cycles quicken. Roles broaden without adjustment. Accountability grows stronger. Authority shifts. Expectations increase. In this environment, leadership identity is not fixed; it is constantly pushed to change, condense, fragment, or dissolve under institutional demands.

Across these chapters, a consistent pattern has emerged. Leaders who remain effective over time do not merely manage change. They anchor themselves within it.

They clarify values even as systems evolve. They maintain professional coherence while responsibilities grow. They guide others through transitions without losing their own footing. They welcome feedback, conflict, and student challenges to strengthen their leadership rather than weaken it.

These capacities redefine endurance.

Endurance isn't emotional toughness. It's coherence — the disciplined alignment of internal conviction and external action in the face of instability. It's the ability to evolve without losing integrity, to expand without scattering, and to carry authority without sacrificing humanity.

Part IV has shown that leadership identity is always changing. It is formed daily through decisions, boundaries, language, reflection, and relational stance. When leaders ignore this internal structure, role fatigue worsens. Professional loneliness grows deeper. Leadership becomes more transactional instead of intentional. Over time, what once felt meaningful starts to seem performative.

When identity is left unsupported, fragmentation follows.

But when leaders intentionally cultivate identity agility, new opportunities arise. Leadership becomes more stable rather than reactive. Transitions shift to be developmental rather than destabilizing. Accountability turns into reflection rather than defensiveness. Authority becomes more integrative rather than isolating. Purpose becomes regenerative rather than depleted.

Yet identity sustainability cannot rest solely on personal discipline.

Throughout this section, a deeper truth has emerged: identity agility is personal work supported by collective design. When institutions broaden expectations without shared planning, identity stress increases. When transitions lack structural support, leaders develop in isolation. When authority expands without shared responsibility, performance replaces coherence.

Partnership safeguards identity from quiet erosion.

It aligns growth with shared expectations. It distributes pressure before it accumulates. It normalizes evolution instead of viewing it as private negotiation.

It structures support across professional shifts.

Leadership that must continually reinvent itself alone eventually fractures. Leadership supported through shared stewardship matures.

Part IV has therefore asked leaders to take responsibility not only for institutional outcomes but also for the integrity of the leadership they demonstrate within those outcomes. Sustainable leadership is intentional. It is built through clarity of values, consistency of boundaries, and disciplined reflection — reinforced by systems that see identity as a leadership asset rather than an afterthought.

This section has strengthened leadership identity.

What remains is integration.

The final part of this book connects the emotional, cultural, and identity themes into a single architectural question: How do we create institutions where sustainability is built into the system rather than seen as heroic? How does leadership shift from personal integrity to collective continuity? How does partnership become standard practice rather than just aspirational language?

Part V answers by shifting from individual durability to institutional design.

From supporting the leader
to supporting the system.

# PART V
## BUILDING CULTURES OF COLLECTIVE CARE AND SUSTAINABLE LEADERSHIP

### Sustainable Leadership Teams on Campus

In higher education, executive leadership teams, dean councils, provost cabinets, and academic senates often operate under ongoing and visible pressure. Budget limits, enrollment fluctuations, accreditation cycles, faculty governance talks, political scrutiny, and public accountability create an environment where decisions have long-term institutional impacts.

These teams are expected to move quickly, stay unified, and handle tension without falling apart. Long hours, high-stakes discussions, and constant crisis management make strain seem normal. Over time, what starts as commitment can turn into exhaustion, emotional isolation, and strategic fatigue.

Collective care models in postsecondary settings strengthen both collaboration and continuity. When executive teams intentionally share emotional containment, clarify distributed authority, and build structures for reflection and recalibration, institutional resilience increases. Sustainable leadership cultures on campus protect both mission and people. They reduce preventable burnout, stabilize succession planning, and preserve intellectual and relational capital across transitions.

In university systems, sustainability is not accidental. It is designed.

## Building Cultures of Collective Care and Sustainable Leadership

If identity agility enables leaders to grow without disappearing, collective care ensures that leadership itself remains a shared endeavor rather than a solitary burden.

For decades, educational leadership has been framed as an individual responsibility—carried quietly, executed competently, and often absorbed at personal cost. Leaders are expected to manage pressure, regulate emotion, maintain clarity, and protect institutional stability even as expectations expand and resources contract. When leaders begin to strain, institutions frequently respond with resilience workshops rather than architectural redesign.

Part V challenges this assumption at its core.

Sustainable leadership isn't driven by exceptional individuals. Instead, it results from systems deliberately designed to share responsibility, emotional labor, authority, and protection. Collective care isn't just sentimentality; it's practical wisdom embedded in structure. It acknowledges that people are the core infrastructure of educational institutions and that when leadership capacity diminishes, institutional coherence declines.

## From Heroic Leadership to Shared Stewardship

Many schools and universities still follow a heroic leadership model—one that values overextension, emphasizes constant availability, and equates sacrifice with dedication. While this approach may ensure short-term stability, it is fundamentally unsustainable.

Heroic leadership relies on concentrated capacity, and when that capacity runs out, systems become unstable.

Collective care replaces heroics with stewardship. It reframes leadership as a distributed function rather than a personal performance. Instead of asking who can endure the most, it asks how responsibility can be structured so endurance is not the primary survival strategy.

Shared stewardship does not weaken accountability. It strengthens it by embedding responsibility into design rather than into personality. It protects leadership continuity by ensuring that stability does not rely on a single individual's stamina.

## Care as a Structural Priority

Care becomes durable only when it is structural.

In many institutions, care relies on generous individuals rather than on reliable systems. When support is driven by personality instead of policies, it becomes inconsistent, fragile, and prone to turnover. Cultural stability varies depending on who holds leadership positions rather than on the structures that define them.

Part V explores how leaders can embed care into institutional structures through intentional practices: distributed leadership teams, formal mentorship pathways, protected reflection spaces, role clarity, succession planning, and communication norms that prioritize recovery alongside productivity. These mechanisms are not peripheral additions. They are protective infrastructure.

When care is designed, burnout decreases. When care is improvised, depletion accelerates.

## Protecting the Protectors

Leaders are frequently the last to receive care. Their roles require steadiness, discretion, and emotional containment, leaving little space for their own processing or support. Over time, this imbalance narrows perspective, weakens presence, and increases isolation.

Collective care acknowledges that those who protect others must also be protected. Sustainable systems refuse to assume unlimited capacity at the top. They design leadership teams that share emotional containment, normalize vulnerability within boundaries, and distribute strategic weight before it concentrates into exhaustion.

When leaders are supported collectively, judgment sharpens, clarity stabilizes, and relational trust deepens. Protection is no longer reactive. It becomes preventative.

## Culture Is Built Through Practice

Culture does not shift through declarations alone. It shifts through repeated patterns of behavior.

Collective care becomes evident in the way meetings are organized, how disagreements are addressed, how mistakes are corrected, how boundaries are upheld, and how recovery is made normal. These everyday practices communicate more than any official statement about values.

When care is practiced consistently, it integrates into institutional identity. When it is missing, no amount of messaging can make up for it.

Culture solidifies through what is repeated.

## Leadership That Lasts

The aim of this final section is not comfort; it is longevity.

Educational institutions require leaders who can remain principled, steady, and effective across years of change. That durability does not arise from personal toughness alone. It emerges from cultures that recognize limitation, value interdependence, and intentionally design for sustainability.

The chapters that follow examine how collective care manifests in mentorship structures, team architecture, distributed authority, and policy alignment that safeguards both people and purpose.

Lasting leadership is not built on sacrifice. It is built on shared responsibility.

In a profession centered on care, collective care is not optional. It is foundational.

## Care as Architecture

Collective care isn't just sentiment; it's a structural responsibility.

It is the intentional redistribution of emotional labor, authority, and protection so that no single person becomes the silent stabilizer of the entire system. Collective care replaces endurance as virtue with sustainability as a guiding principle. It shifts leadership culture away from heroic overfunctioning and towards shared stewardship embedded within institutional structures.

Mentorship structures, shared leadership teams, distributed authority, and aligned policies are not just fringe elements of culture; they are its foundation. They shape whether leadership sustainability relies on personal sacrifice or deliberate planning. When care is viewed as merely personality, burnout becomes foreseeable. When care is intentionally organized, stability endures.

The final part of this book isn't about adding another initiative to overburdened systems. It's about fundamentally redesigning how leadership operates. Partnership isn't just a gentle addition to authority; it is the key that sustains authority. It guarantees that responsibility builds strength instead of creating division and that protection is shared rather than silently taken in.

Collective care distinguishes systems that merely survive reform cycles from those that endure beyond them. Endurance alone cannot stabilize institutions. Architecture can.

## Partnership Lens

Collective care isn't just an emotional choice; it's a shared responsibility built into design. What looks like burnout is often a result of concentrated authority and unshared strain. Leadership lasts when stewardship is organized rather than assumed, and when responsibility is spread out before pressure builds up. Sustainable cultures aren't maintained by extraordinary individuals alone but by systems that prevent care from being a solitary task.

# CHAPTER 18

## COLLECTIVE CARE AS A STRUCTURAL LEADERSHIP PRIORITY

### Global Leadership Spotlight

**Country Focus: Norway**
**Collective Care as Infrastructure**

Norway's education system functions within a broader social framework that emphasizes collective responsibility, educator well-being, and institutional sustainability. National labor policies, education governance structures, and school leadership models focus on work-life balance, collaborative decision-making, and shared accountability. Teachers and school leaders benefit from systems designed to protect professional capacity through reasonable workload expectations, structured support services, and coordinated leadership teams.

This approach demonstrates that long-term educational quality relies on sustainable working conditions rather than individual endurance. When care is integrated into institutional design, leaders are not forced to offset systemic strain through personal sacrifice. Instead, they are backed by policies and structures that foster stability, continuity, and career longevity.

Norway's experience illustrates a broader leadership principle: care does not weaken performance—it enhances it. When collective care is integrated into system design, leaders are better equipped to maintain clarity, consistency, and long-term effectiveness. Structural support helps leadership stay steady rather than reactive, allowing institutions to focus on growth instead of crisis management.

**Leadership Reflection:**

What structural changes would be required in your organization to treat care as leadership infrastructure rather than an optional initiative?

Care must be embedded, not optional.

In many educational institutions, care is seen as an individual responsibility. When people face challenges, they are encouraged to practice self-care, attend wellness sessions, or build personal resilience. While these supports can be helpful, they shift the responsibility for sustainability onto individuals rather than onto the systems that shape their daily experiences.

This chapter advocates for a major shift: moving from care as a personal coping mechanism to collective care as a key leadership focus. Sustainable leadership doesn't ask people to endure more; it creates environments that support human capacity while achieving institutional goals.

## Collective Care Versus Individual Coping

Individual coping assumes that stress is an unavoidable part of meaningful work and that people need to adapt accordingly. Collective care recognizes that much of what drains educators is not inherent to the work itself, but to how the work is organized, paced, and supported.

When leaders rely mainly on individual coping strategies, they inadvertently normalize conditions that cause harm. People learn to deal with overload privately rather than question whether it's necessary. Over time, this weakens trust and supports a culture where struggle is seen as personal and success as performative.

Collective care redefines sustainability as a shared responsibility. It questions how leadership decisions impact workload, emotional labor, and recovery—not just outcomes. This perspective does not lessen accountability; it connects accountability with human experience.

## Structural Compassion in Leadership Design

Structural compassion is care made visible through design.

It is reflected in how schedules are constructed, how initiatives are layered, how expectations are communicated, and how recovery is normalized. Compassion at this level is not sentimental. It is strategic.

Leaders practicing structural compassion examine where systems unintentionally demand constant urgency, emotional suppression, or overfunctioning. They question assumptions that equate productivity with effectiveness and challenge practices that reward endurance over sustainability.

Structural compassion also includes anticipating impact. Before making changes, leaders think not just about how to improve results, but also about what will be needed emotionally and relationally from those doing the work.

This foresight protects both people and progress.

## Policies That Protect People

Policies communicate values more clearly than mission statements.

When policies focus on results without considering capacity, they send a clear message: people come second. On the other hand, policies that protect individuals—through fair workload expectations, transparent decision-making, and flexibility—show that human well-being is essential for institutional success.

Protective policies do not remove challenges or high standards. They clarify boundaries by defining what is expected and what is not. They set guardrails to prevent burnout from becoming the norm.

Examples of protective design include clear limits on initiative overload, explicit expectations around availability, and feedback processes that do not penalize honesty. These policies reduce ambiguity and enable people to engage fully without fear of hidden costs.

## Care as Infrastructure

Care becomes sustainable when it is treated as infrastructure rather than intention.

Just as schools invest in physical safety and instructional resources, they must also invest in relational and emotional sustainability. This includes leadership development that addresses emotional labor, systems for peer support, and structures that prevent leaders from becoming isolated.

When care is infrastructural, it does not depend on goodwill. It is reliable, equitable, and consistent.

## The Leadership Shift Required

Structural embedding of care requires leaders to challenge long-standing norms. It involves moving from crisis-driven decision-making to deliberate pacing. It also calls for recognizing limits without equating them with weakness.

This shift can seem countercultural in environments that value urgency and sacrifice. However, leaders who oppose it often end up dealing with preventable burnout, turnover, and disengagement.

Collective care isn't about comfort; it's about maintaining capacity.

## From Optional to Essential

When care is seen as optional, it is unevenly distributed, with those who have less power or fewer resources bearing the highest costs. When care becomes a fundamental part of the system, it strengthens the system's integrity. This chapter urges leaders to integrate care into how schools and institutions operate—not as a wellness program but as a leadership priority equal to performance and accountability. Care must be embedded into the system instead of being optional because systems that rely on individuals to cope eventually break down under their own weight.

The upcoming chapters will explore how collective care is practiced through mentorship, team organization, and leadership frameworks that protect those who serve others. Lasting leadership understands this truth: people are not renewable resources.

# INSIDE THE CLASSROOM

## When Care Became Collective

During a particularly demanding semester, the leadership team noticed an increase in sick days, shortened tempers, and quiet withdrawal among staff. Instead of launching another wellness initiative, they made a small but intentional structural shift.

Meeting schedules were adjusted to reduce overload. Coverage systems were redesigned to prevent the same individuals from carrying repeated substitutions. Communication expectations were clarified to protect evenings and weekends.

The change was subtle, but the impact was noticeable. Teachers lingered longer in hallways. Conversations softened. The emotional climate began to stabilize.

Care became visible not through slogans, but through design.

Collective care is not about asking people to be kinder to one another. It is about building systems that protect human capacity. When care becomes structural, sustainability stops being aspirational and becomes operational.

# LEADERSHIP NEXT STEPS —
## Collective Care as Infrastructure

 **Awareness Shift: Recognize Care as Organizational Design, Not Individual Effort**

Care in schools is often seen as personal kindness or individual wellness practices. While relational compassion is important, sustainable leadership requires a wider structural perspective. Collective care must be recognized as part of organizational infrastructure — integrated into policies, schedules, leadership norms, workload design, and institutional expectations.

Begin examining where care is informally carried by a small number of emotionally engaged leaders or staff rather than supported through intentional systems. These patterns reveal where institutions rely on personal goodwill instead of structural responsibility.

**Ask yourself:**

Where is care viewed as optional instead of a vital part of the organization?

 **Leadership Behavior Adjustment: Model Collective Care Leadership**

Leaders communicate organizational priorities through daily leadership behavior far more powerfully than through formal statements. When leaders consistently protect time, capacity, and relational well-being, care becomes normalized rather than symbolic.

Leaders model collective care when they:

- Protect staff workload boundaries rather than rewarding overextension
- Encourage recovery and rest without attaching stigma or guilt

- Address burnout patterns proactively rather than waiting for a crisis.
- Integrate human capacity considerations into operational decision-making

When leaders demonstrate care through concrete action, institutional culture begins to recalibrate around sustainability rather than survival.

 **Structural or Cultural Reinforcement: Build Care Into Institutional Systems**

Collective care becomes durable only when embedded into formal structure. Without institutional reinforcement, well-being initiatives remain fragmented, temporary, and dependent on individual leadership personalities.

Identify one system-level adjustment that strengthens care infrastructure, such as:

- Redesigning schedules to allow cognitive and emotional recovery
- Establishing leadership policies that protect sustainable workload expectations
- Building peer support and collective care practices into organizational design
- Aligning performance standards with realistic human capacity

When care is structurally supported, resilience becomes institutional rather than individual.

## Leadership Anchor: Design Systems That Carry People, Not Just Performance

Leadership that emphasizes collective care does not weaken standards — it reinforces them. When organizations are built to support human capacity, individuals can contribute more consistently, creatively, and with greater long-term dedication. Collective care is not just an emotional addition to leadership; it is the structural foundation enabling organizations to operate effectively without risking the well-being of those who sustain them.

## Partnership as Leadership Architecture

Care should be integrated rather than improvised. When protection is focused in a single role, depletion becomes predictable. Partnership intentionally redistributes authority and emotional labor rather than relying on necessity. Stability arises from shared stewardship.

# CHAPTER 19

## MENTORSHIP MODELS FOR EMOTIONAL LEADERSHIP DEVELOPMENT

### Global Leadership Spotlight

#### Country Focus: Ghana
#### Mentorship and Leadership Development

Ghana has undertaken ongoing efforts to enhance teacher development and leadership skills through expanded professional development programs, mentorship initiatives, and instructional coaching models. National education strategies highlight the importance of continuous professional learning to boost teaching quality, improve retention, and develop leadership pipelines within schools and districts. These initiatives reflect a growing understanding that leadership capacity must be deliberately cultivated rather than assumed.

Structured mentorship programs connect experienced educators with early-career teachers and emerging leaders, fostering opportunities for knowledge sharing, professional growth, and leadership development. This strategy supports both individual progress and institutional stability. When mentorship is integrated into system design, it reduces isolation, speeds up professional development, and enhances long-term workforce stability.

Ghana's experience emphasizes accompaniment as a leadership strategy. Leaders are not developed through evaluation alone—they grow through guided practice, reflection, and relational support. Sustainable leadership systems invest in people by creating pathways for development that span across different stages of a career.

**Leadership Reflection:**

Who is responsible for developing emerging leaders in your organization, and what structures are in place to ensure mentorship is consistent, supported, and sustainable?

Mentorship is not advice—it is accompaniment.

In education, mentorship is often seen as simply transferring knowledge from experienced individuals to those who are less experienced. While guidance is important, this narrow view overlooks the deeper role mentorship can play in emotionally complex systems. When leadership calls for regulation, reflection, and adaptability in identity, mentorship should go beyond just instruction and focus on building relationships.

This chapter examines mentorship as a structural approach that builds emotional leadership skills throughout different career stages. It presents mentorship not as a way to solve problems, but as ongoing support during growth, transition, and uncertainty.

## Mentorship as Emotional Infrastructure

Effective mentorship provides more than answers. It offers containment.

In settings where educators are expected to quietly handle emotional burdens, mentorship becomes one of the few spaces where complexity can be recognized without penalty. When intentionally designed, mentorship functions as emotional infrastructure—supporting reflection, normalization, and integration.

This infrastructure is especially crucial in systems where pace and pressure limit processing time. Without mentorship, educators must navigate identity challenges and leadership development on their own. With mentorship, learning becomes relational instead of isolating.

## Supporting New Teachers Without Overwhelm

New teachers often start their careers with enthusiasm and idealism, along with uncertainty and fear. They are managing not only instructional challenges but also the emotional aspects of classroom management, student needs, and institutional culture.

Mentorship for new teachers must focus on emotional regulation as much as pedagogy. New educators benefit from mentors who normalize struggle without downplaying standards, help them interpret institutional expectations, and model a sustainable professional identity rather than heroic endurance.

Accompaniment at this stage involves listening first, giving contextualized feedback, and helping new teachers integrate their personal identity with role expectations. When mentorship only focuses on performance, emotional burnout rises. When it also supports identity, retention and growth improve.

## Developing Emerging Leaders with Integrity

Emerging leaders face a unique set of challenges. They are often asked to take on influence before they feel fully ready, navigating changing relationships and rising visibility. The emotional complexity of this transition is rarely directly addressed.

Mentorship for emerging leaders must provide space for identity negotiation. These leaders need support not only in decision-making but also in boundary-setting, emotional regulation, and ethical clarity. They benefit from mentors who can discuss ambiguity without offering premature certainty.

Accompaniment here means walking alongside leaders as they learn to hold authority without defensiveness and responsibility without self-erasure. It helps emerging leaders integrate their leadership identity gradually rather than perform it prematurely.

## Accompanying Veteran Educators Through Transition

Veteran educators navigating transition—whether role changes, shifting expectations, or reevaluating their career paths—often face a unique kind of isolation. Their experience is assumed to be full of confidence, while their doubts are overlooked.

Mentorship at this stage should honor accumulated wisdom while recognizing the stress of change. Experienced educators benefit from support that affirms their contributions and helps them recalibrate without judgment.

This mentorship is not remedial; it is renewal-focused. It helps experienced professionals reflect on their changing identity, redefine their purpose, and stay engaged without taking on the full burden of the institution.

## Designing Mentorship for Emotional Leadership

Emotionally intelligent mentorship does not happen accidentally. It requires intentional design.

Effective models focus on consistency rather than intensity, on reflection rather than prescription, and on relationships rather than hierarchy. They set clear expectations for both mentor and mentee, shielding the relationship from becoming transactional or extractive.

Importantly, mentorship needs adequate resources. Time, training, and recognition are crucial. When mentorship depends only on goodwill, it repeats the same patterns of invisible labor that harm sustainability.

## The Leader's Role in Mentorship Culture

Leaders influence mentorship culture by their actions and structural support. When leaders see mentorship as optional, it remains fragile. When they integrate it into career development, it becomes transformative.

Leadership responsibility involves supporting mentors without overburdening them. It also includes developing multiple mentorship pathways, understanding that no single relationship can fulfill all needs.

## Mentorship as Collective Care in Action

Mentorship facilitates collective care. It spreads wisdom, normalizes challenges, and decreases isolation throughout the system. It supports individuals in their growth without them having to carry the workload alone.

This chapter does not depict mentorship as a program to be carried out. Instead, it describes mentorship as a leadership commitment—to stand alongside people as they grow emotionally and professionally.

Mentorship isn't advice; it's companionship.

And in educational systems characterized by change, accompaniment might be the most effective form of leadership growth available.

The final chapters will examine how these principles apply to team design, the protection of leaders, and the embedding of emotional leadership into institutional culture—ensuring that care and sustainability are built into the structure, not just goals.

# INSIDE THE CLASSROOM

### The Mentor Who Stayed

A first-year teacher sat quietly in the back of a professional development session, overwhelmed by information and unsure where to start. Later, a veteran educator approached and simply said, "You don't have to figure this out alone."

Over the following months, they met regularly. Not just to discuss lesson planning, but to talk about confidence, boundaries, and the emotional weight of teaching. The mentor did not offer perfect answers. Instead, they offered presence.

What made the difference was not expertise. It was consistency.

Mentorship isn't just a program requirement; it's a relational commitment. When executed effectively, it becomes one of the most powerful tools for leadership development and retention. It shows that growth is supported, not something to be survived alone.

## LEADERSHIP NEXT STEPS —
## Mentorship and Leadership Development

 **Awareness Shift: Recognize Mentorship as Leadership Infrastructure**

Mentorship is often seen as informal support or voluntary relationship-building. While personal connection is important, sustainable emotional leadership growth needs mentorship to be viewed as part of institutional infrastructure. Without deliberate design, leadership development becomes uneven, relying on access, proximity, or personality rather than organizational commitment.

Start analyzing where leadership development depends on individual effort rather than clear pathways. These gaps show where emerging leaders are left to handle emotional complexity, role expectations, and career growth without support.

**Ask yourself:**

Where is leadership development dependent on chance rather than design?

## Leadership Behavior Adjustment: Model Developmental Leadership Presence

Leaders shape learning culture through how they invest in others. Developmental leadership requires time, intentional attention, and relational consistency. It moves beyond evaluation toward growth-oriented engagement.

Leaders model mentorship-centered leadership when they:

- Prioritize regular developmental conversations rather than only performance feedback
- Share leadership experience and decision-making rationale transparently
- Provide emotional guidance alongside technical coaching
- Support reflective practice rather than transactional supervision

When leaders invest relationally in development, leadership capacity expands across the organization.

## Structural or Cultural Reinforcement: Build Sustainable Mentorship Systems

Mentorship is only scalable and sustainable when integrated into organizational systems. Without a clear structure, mentorship stays fragile and inconsistent.

Identify one system-level practice that strengthens mentorship infrastructure, such as:

- Creating formal mentorship pathways for emerging leaders
- Establishing leadership learning cohorts
- Integrating mentorship into promotion and succession planning
- Allocating protected time for developmental leadership work

When mentorship is structurally supported, leadership development becomes institutional rather than individual.

### Leadership Anchor: Grow Leaders Without Creating Dependency

Effective mentorship does not create followers — it builds independent, emotionally grounded leaders. Sustainable mentorship equips individuals with clarity, confidence, and professional identity rather than dependence on authority figures. When leadership development is designed to empower rather than control, organizations gain depth of leadership capacity that endures beyond any single generation.

## Partnership as Leadership Architecture

Mentorship prevents leadership from turning into lonely endurance. Without support, stress solidifies into quiet isolation. Partnership formalizes guidance across different career levels and leadership stages. Growth speeds up when wisdom is shared instead of hoarded.

# CHAPTER 20

## SUSTAINABLE LEADERSHIP TEAMS: PROTECTING THE PROTECTORS

### Global Leadership Spotlight

**Country Focus: Chile**
**Sustainable Leadership Teams**

Chile's education system has undergone significant decentralization reforms, shifting more decision-making, resource management, and instructional leadership power to schools and local education authorities. As a result, school leaders now bear greater responsibility not only for academic results but also for organizational culture, staff development, and community engagement. This expanded range of duties has made collaborative leadership models essential rather than optional.

In decentralized systems, leadership effectiveness depends less on individual authority and more on team cohesion. Leadership teams must coordinate strategy, share decision-making, and distribute operational and emotional responsibilities across roles. When leadership is concentrated in a single position, workload and burnout tend to rise. When responsibility is shared intentionally, leaders can better sustain performance and keep organizational stability.

Chile's experience underscores the importance of team integrity. Sustainable leadership teams depend on trust, clear roles, open communication, and shared responsibility. When teams work with cohesion, they become sources of renewal instead of exhaustion. Collective leadership capacity enhances both institutional resilience and long-term effectiveness.

**Leadership Reflection:**

How is leadership responsibility distributed across teams in your organization, and where might clearer role design or shared decision-making improve sustainability?

Those who hold others need protection, too.

Educational leadership is often viewed as a position of authority. In reality, it functions more as a position of containment. Leaders handle uncertainty, regulate emotions, manage conflicts, and make decisions that have emotional effects far beyond their offices. When this workload is concentrated rather than shared, burnout at the top becomes not just possible but expected.

This chapter explores how leadership teams can intentionally be structured to share emotional burdens, safeguard decision-makers, and maintain leadership capacity over time. Sustainable leadership isn't about individual endurance; it is built through team frameworks that acknowledge emotional labor as genuine work.

## Leadership Teams as Emotional Systems

Leadership teams do not function only as operational units. They function as emotional systems.

How information flows, how disagreement is handled, and how responsibility is distributed all influence whether leaders feel supported or isolated. In many schools and organizations, leadership teams are designed for efficiency rather than sustainability. Tasks are assigned, decisions are delegated, but emotional burdens remain unaddressed.

Over time, this creates predictable roles. One leader becomes the emotional support. Another acts as the crisis responder. Yet another holds institutional memory. These roles may never be officially named, but they influence how stress develops.

When emotional roles are implicit instead of intentional, imbalance ensues. Some leaders overextend themselves while others withdraw. Burnout remains hidden and localized until it becomes unavoidable.

## Designing Teams That Share the Weight

Sustainable leadership teams are designed with distribution in mind.

This doesn't mean the workload is consistent all the time. It means intentionally rotating emotional responsibility and clearly defining who is responsible for what. Leaders benefit from having open conversations about capacity, boundaries, and support—discussions that are often avoided in the name of professionalism.

When teams openly name emotional roles, they gain flexibility. Leaders can step up when they have capacity and step back when they do not. This transparency reduces shame and prevents silent overload.

Designing for sustainability also requires aligning authority with responsibility. Leaders expected to handle emotional labor must have enough influence to impact the situation. Without this alignment, frustration and fatigue build up quickly.

## Emotional Load Distribution as Leadership Practice

Emotional load involves making decisions amid uncertainty, managing conflict, handling community anger, and supporting staff through distress without immediate solutions. This burden is often unevenly shared, depending on temperament, experience, or role.

Effective leadership teams actively monitor this distribution. They check not only on tasks completed but also on the stress levels carried. They recognize when one leader consistently takes on more tension and make adjustments accordingly.

This calls for a cultural shift. Emotional check-ins should become a normal part of professional practice instead of being seen as personal disclosure. Teams that treat emotional load as valid data make better decisions and stay clear-headed under pressure.

## Preventing Burnout at the Top

Burnout among leaders is often concealed by their competence. Leaders continue to perform long after their capacity has been exceeded, driven by responsibility and loyalty. By the time burnout becomes apparent, the damage has usually already occurred.

Preventing burnout requires proactive planning rather than reactive support. Leadership teams must incorporate regular opportunities for reflection, peer consultation, and recalibration. These spaces enable leaders to process complexity before it becomes harmful.

Leaders also need permission to be human. When leadership culture equates strength with emotional invisibility, burnout becomes inevitable. Teams that model vulnerability without collapsing create psychological safety for sustainable leadership.

## Protecting Leaders Without Diluting Authority

There's a common fear that protecting leaders will weaken their authority. In reality, unsupported leaders are much more likely to react impulsively, withdraw emotionally, or leave their roles entirely. Protection doesn't mean shielding from challenges or avoiding responsibility. It means ensuring leaders don't have to handle complexity, conflict, and responsibility all by themselves.

When leaders are protected, they become clearer, more steady, and more effective. They are better equipped to handle conflict without becoming consumed by it and to make tough decisions without taking backlash personally. This kind of support strengthens authority rather than weakening it, enabling leadership to be exercised with calmness, sound judgment, and a focus on long-term goals.

## Leadership Team Integrity

Sustainable leadership teams operate with integrity, not perfection. Integrity shows in how teams handle misalignment, repair after conflict, and hold each other accountable without blame or shame. It depends on trust that develops over time through consistency, transparency, and shared responsibility.

When leadership teams operate with integrity, they become sources of renewal rather than exhaustion. Instead of draining emotional energy, they replenish it. In these environments, leaders are not only supported—they are empowered, enabling the whole system to thrive through more stable leadership and better decision-making.

## From Individual Heroics to Collective Strength

This chapter urges leaders to shift from heroic leadership stories to focusing on collective strength. Protecting those who protect us is not self-indulgent; it is vital.

Educational systems cannot be sustained by leaders who are quietly breaking under the weight of supporting others. Leadership teams must be designed to handle complexity together—sharing emotional burdens, offering support, and exemplifying the care they aim to foster throughout the institution.

Those who serve others also need protection. When leaders are supported, their leadership lasts.

The final chapter will unify this work—examining how emotionally intelligent leadership becomes part of school and district culture, making sure that care, integrity, and sustainability are embedded in the very fabric of the institution rather than depending on individuals.

# INSIDE THE CLASSROOM

## Protecting the Protectors

During a leadership retreat, one assistant principal finally expressed what others had been quietly feeling: "We are good at protecting everyone else. We are not good at protecting ourselves."

The room went quiet. Heads nodded.

They started redesigning how leadership duties were allocated. Decision-making became more intentional and shared. Emotional labor was recognized rather than assumed. Backup systems were established to ensure no one had to handle crisis management alone.

Over time, the team felt steadier. Less reactive. More collaborative.

Sustainable leadership teams are based on shared responsibility, mutual support, and purposeful planning.

---

## LEADERSHIP NEXT STEPS —
## Sustainable Leadership Teams

**1  Awareness Shift: Recognize Leadership Teams as High-Risk Sustainability Zones**

Leadership teams often serve as emotional shock absorbers for organizations. They handle crisis response, decision-making pressure, relational conflicts, and accountability demands while staying publicly composed. When this burden remains unexamined, leadership teams quietly become centers of burnout rather than sources of stability.

Start evaluating where leadership teams are functioning in constant urgency mode without sufficient recovery, reflection, or mutual support. These patterns show where institutional expectations are surpassing sustainable leadership capacity.

**Ask yourself:**

Where are leadership teams expected to protect the system without being protected themselves?

 **Leadership Behavior Adjustment: Practice Mutual Leadership Care**

Sustainable leadership does not rely on individual resilience alone. It is built through collective responsibility among leadership peers. Leaders must move beyond parallel leadership and into shared emotional and professional support.

Leadership teams model mutual care when they:

- Normalize honest dialogue about leadership strain
- Share decision burden rather than concentrating pressure
- Check in on capacity, not just performance
- Offer peer support without hierarchy or competition

When leadership teams support each other intentionally, institutional stability becomes stronger.

 **Structural or Cultural Reinforcement: Design Team Sustainability Systems**

Leadership sustainability cannot depend on informal goodwill. It must be structurally reinforced. Without intentional design, leadership teams absorb pressure without institutional protection.

Identify one system-level practice that strengthens leadership team sustainability, such as:

- Creating protected time for leadership reflection and alignment
- Establishing rotating leadership responsibilities to reduce overload
- Building peer coaching or leadership supervision structures

- Aligning leadership expectations with realistic workload capacity

When leadership teams are structurally supported, protection becomes systemic rather than personal.

---

## Leadership Anchor: Protect the Protectors to Preserve the System

Institutions often rely on leadership teams to stabilize culture, handle crises, and ensure continuity. When those leaders lack support, the entire system becomes vulnerable. Sustainable leadership involves creating environments where leadership teams are not expected to sacrifice themselves to support others. Protecting the protectors is not a luxury — it is a strategic necessity that ensures the institution's long-term stability.

## Partnership as Leadership Architecture 

Those who support others need support themselves. Protection can't rely solely on personal strength. Partnerships create leadership teams that share emotional support and strategic responsibility. Sustainability happens when protectors are protected together.

# CHAPTER 21

## EMBEDDING EMOTIONAL LEADERSHIP INTO SCHOOL AND DISTRICT CULTURE

### Global Leadership Spotlight

**Country Focus: UNESCO SDG 4 (Global Framework)**
**Embedding Emotional Leadership Systemically**

UNESCO's Sustainable Development Goal 4 (SDG 4) commits countries to ensuring inclusive, equitable, and high-quality education and to expanding lifelong learning opportunities for all by 2030. This worldwide framework stresses access, literacy, learning outcomes, and workforce readiness across different national contexts. Governments, education ministries, and international organizations have aligned policies and funding strategies around these targets, recognizing education as a key driver of social and economic progress.

While SDG 4 focuses on measurable results, reaching these goals relies on more than just curriculum changes and infrastructure investments. It requires leadership structures capable of maintaining human capacity over time. Educational transformation depends on leaders who can manage complexity, drive change, support staff well-being, and keep institutional stability under pressure. Without emotionally sustainable leadership, reform efforts risk being brief or uneven in implementation.

This global framework sees emotional leadership as essential rather than optional. When emotional intelligence, relational leadership, and collective care are included in policy making, leadership development, and organizational design, education systems become more resilient. Sustainable reform depends not only on what leaders do but also on how leadership itself is structured.

**Leadership Reflection:**

How does your leadership model support long-term system sustainability by protecting human capacity while advancing performance and reform goals?

Sustainability requires alignment.

Emotionally intelligent leadership cannot depend solely on individual leaders, personal values, or informal practices. When leadership based on emotional integrity exists only in isolated pockets, it remains fragile—prone to turnover, policy shifts, and competing priorities. For leadership to be sustainable, it must be embedded in the cultures of schools and districts, rather than relying on a few dedicated individuals.

This chapter explores how emotionally intelligent leadership becomes systemic. It investigates alignment across policy, leadership development, and long-term culture-building to ensure that care, clarity, and sustainability are reinforced at every level of the organization.

## From Leadership Style to Leadership Standard

In many institutions, emotional leadership is seen as a leadership style—something some leaders naturally embody while others may lack. This perspective restricts its influence. Styles differ, but standards remain.

Embedding emotional leadership requires shifting from preference to expectation. Emotional integrity, cultural flexibility, and identity agility must be clearly reflected in how leadership is defined, evaluated, and supported. When these capacities are explicitly named, they become standard rather than optional.

This does not mean enforcing emotional uniformity. It means clarifying what responsible leadership looks like in emotionally complex environments and aligning systems accordingly.

## Policy Integration as Cultural Signal

Policies are among the most powerful cultural signals an institution sends. They communicate what is prioritized, protected, and measured.

When policies focus solely on outcomes without considering process or impact, they foster a culture of urgency and extraction. When policies include emotional factors—such as workload limits, communication expectations, and decision-making procedures—they convey that human sustainability is important.

Policy integration involves evaluating existing frameworks through an emotional leadership perspective. Leaders consider not only whether a policy is effective but also if it is sustainable. They assess how policies influence trust, emotional burden, and long-term engagement.

Policies that safeguard time for reflection, promote transparent communication, and define boundaries decrease ambiguity and foster emotionally responsible leadership.

## Leadership Pipelines That Build Capacity

Leadership pipelines shape the future of organizations. When pipelines focus only on technical skills and performance metrics, they develop leaders who are operationally capable but emotionally unprepared.

Embedding emotional leadership demands a rethink of leadership development. Training must focus on emotional regulation, identity reflection, conflict management, and cultural awareness as essential skills—not optional topics.

Mentorship, coaching, and peer learning should be structured to support emotional development across various career stages. This ensures that emerging leaders assume roles with understanding rather than solely depending on trial and error.

Pipelines that integrate emotional leadership decrease burnout, enhance decision-making, and boost retention across all levels.

## Alignment Across Levels

Culture is built through consistency.

When district leadership models emotional integrity but site-level leaders lack support, misalignment happens. When schools try to practice collective care without policy backing, sustainability weakens.

Embedding emotional leadership requires alignment across levels—district, school, and classroom. Expectations, resources, and accountability must reinforce one another.

This alignment does not require uniform implementation. It requires shared principles and mutual reinforcement. Leaders at every level must understand how emotional leadership shows up in their specific context and how it connects to the larger system.

## Long-Term Cultural Change

Cultural change occurs through consistent practice rather than declarations.

Embedding emotional leadership requires patience. Leaders must be willing to reinforce expectations consistently, revisit decisions when impact becomes clear, and adjust course without abandoning values.

Long-term change also requires measuring beyond traditional metrics. Institutions must learn to evaluate trust, engagement, and sustainability—not as abstract ideals, but as signs of organizational health.

When emotional leadership is embedded, it becomes self-reinforcing. New leaders are socialized into the culture. Practices are maintained through transitions. The system retains coherence even under pressure.

## Leadership Beyond Individuals

This chapter emphasizes a key truth of sustainable leadership: no one person can shape culture alone. Emotionally intelligent leadership must be embedded within structures, policies, and shared practices. When this happens, leaders are freed from heroic overreach and are better supported in performing their roles with clarity and consistency.

Embedding emotional leadership is an ongoing commitment, not a final step—it demands vigilance, reflection, and alignment as contexts change. Sustainability relies on coherence between values and systems. When leadership priorities are reinforced structurally, culture becomes resilient instead of fragile.

The conclusion that follows will round out this work by examining the next generation of school leadership and the type of leaders our systems need to develop to remain human, effective, and whole during times of significant change. Because lasting leadership is not improvised; it is deliberate.

# INSIDE THE CLASSROOM

## When Culture Finally Shifted

The changes didn't happen overnight. There wasn't a single announcement that changed the school's culture. Instead, the shift happened gradually. Leaders became more consistent in their presence. Communication improved in clarity. Emotional honesty felt safer. Policies started to better reflect the stated values.

Staff observed the difference not in slogans but in daily interactions—how meetings were conducted, how conflicts were addressed, and how leadership responded during stress. Culture changed not because of a single initiative but because leadership behavior became consistent, relational, and human-focused. Sustainable change is rarely sudden; it is cumulative, developed through repetition, presence, and alignment over time.

---

# LEADERSHIP NEXT STEPS —
## Embedding Emotional Leadership Systemically

 **Awareness Shift: Recognize Emotional Leadership as Institutional Architecture**

Emotional leadership is often viewed as a personal leadership skill or personality trait. In reality, it should be understood as part of institutional structure — embedded in policies, professional development, leadership expectations, and cultural norms. When emotional leadership depends on individual leaders, it becomes fragile and inconsistent.

Begin analyzing how emotionally intelligent practices depend on personal initiative rather than organizational structure. These gaps expose areas where leadership culture is at risk of regression when personnel change.

**Ask yourself:**

Where is emotional leadership practiced informally instead of embedded structurally?

 **Leadership Behavior Adjustment: Model Emotionally Intelligent Systems Leadership**

System-level emotional leadership requires leaders to go beyond individual influence and focus on cultural stewardship. Leaders must demonstrate emotional integrity not only in relationships but also in how they design processes, communicate priorities, and make decisions that impact entire communities.

Leaders demonstrate systems-level emotional leadership when they:

- Integrate emotional considerations into strategic planning
- Communicate change with transparency and empathy
- Prioritize relational trust alongside operational efficiency
- Align leadership behavior with stated cultural values

When leaders demonstrate emotional leadership at the organizational level, culture starts to stabilize around shared norms instead of individual influence.

 **Structural or Cultural Reinforcement: Institutionalize Emotional Leadership Practices**

For emotional leadership to last, it must be integrated into formal organizational structures. Without institutional support, emotionally healthy leadership stays aspirational rather than practical.

Identify one system-level practice that strengthens emotional leadership infrastructure, such as:

- Embedding emotional leadership competencies into leadership standards
- Integrating emotional intelligence training into professional development pipelines
- Aligning evaluation systems with relational leadership outcomes
- Creating accountability structures that support emotionally responsible leadership

When emotional leadership is institutionalized, it becomes sustainable across leadership transitions and reform cycles.

## Leadership Anchor: Build Systems That Carry Emotional Leadership Forward

Emotional leadership is not sustained through individual excellence alone. It endures when institutions are intentionally designed to protect relational health, leadership integrity, and collective capacity. When emotional leadership is embedded systemically, schools and districts move beyond reactive leadership and toward cultures that can adapt, recover, and thrive over time. This is how leadership becomes legacy rather than personality.

## Partnership as Leadership Architecture

Leadership values must endure beyond individual personalities. When care stays personal instead of becoming structural, culture reverts under pressure. Partnership weaves stewardship into policy, pipelines, and succession planning. Endurance becomes institutional when responsibility is intentionally shared.

## Final Synthesis

### From Emotional Weight to Leadership Legacy

This book started by recognizing what many educational leaders quietly face: systemic exhaustion, ongoing emotional labor, identity challenges, and cultural pressures that go well beyond instructional leadership. It argued from the beginning that leadership fatigue is not just personal burnout. It is the expected result of systems that demand stability without redesign, resilience without relief, and high performance without structural safeguards.

From the beginning, the core message has been clear and intentional: sustainability in leadership isn't achieved through endurance alone. Instead, it is built through emotional integrity, structural accountability, shared partnership, and collective care integrated into institutional design.

Part I explored the emotional structure of modern education. Exhaustion was reframed not as weakness but as organizational feedback. Identity erosion was seen as a professional risk rather than a personal flaw. The excessive use of resilience language was analyzed critically. The hidden emotional currents influencing school culture were brought to light. These chapters did not focus on discouragement; they brought clarity. They shifted the story from silent endurance to informed awareness, from individual coping to systemic understanding.

Part II shifted from diagnosis to disciplined response. Emotional integrity was positioned as a stabilizing leadership skill under ongoing pressure. Leaders were encouraged to anchor rather than absorb, to coach without adding more strain, to hold space without losing structure, and to rebuild trust through transparent accountability instead of reputational management. Emotional leadership was redefined not as temperament but as a professional practice.

This section also marked a key shift in leadership thinking: moving from authority based on position to collaboration. Sustainable systems don't rely on hierarchy alone. They last when leaders work with those they lead to analyze conditions, share responsibility, and redesign structural issues. Partnership changes feedback from simply evaluating to co-creating solutions. It shifts leadership focus from "Who needs to improve?" to "What needs to be restructured?" In this way, it reduces pressure concentrated in one area and restores dignity throughout the system.

Part III expanded leadership outward into collective culture. Generational tension, community context, cultural flexibility, equity implementation, and inclusion were reframed as structural leadership responsibilities rather than interpersonal conflicts. Culture was examined not as rhetoric but as reinforcement — shaped by systems, behavioral patterns, and the distribution of emotional labor. When responsibility concentrates, fragility accelerates. When responsibility is intentionally shared, stability strengthens. Partnership transforms difference from disruption into shared design.

Part IV returned inward not to focus on the self, but to protect continuity. Leadership identity, professional belonging, transitions, reflective accountability, and collective care were seen as foundational elements rather than optional practices. Identity agility was described as the ability to evolve without losing integrity — to adapt without breaking coherence. Leadership was viewed not only as guiding change but as maintaining alignment within change. Without coherence, reform cycles drain leaders faster than they strengthen institutions. With shared stewardship, identity matures instead of fragmenting.

Together, these movements form a coherent leadership arc:

From awareness to integrity.

From positional authority to shared partnership.

From individual posture to collective culture.

From endurance to sustainability.

From reaction to intentional design.

The argument that emerges is both simple and demanding.

Leadership doesn't fail because leaders care too deeply. It falters when systems rely on care without providing support. Leadership isn't weakened because individuals are fragile. It breaks down when responsibility is centralized instead of shared. Leadership doesn't lose credibility because standards are high. It loses credibility when humanity is treated as optional.

The future of educational leadership won't rely on harder effort alone. Instead, it will depend on smarter design—emotionally intelligent systems, relational accountability, and structures that safeguard those entrusted with leading. Leadership will develop when evaluation gives way to collaboration, when endurance is replaced by redesign, and when partnership becomes a practical goal rather than just an ideal.

This is the work beyond the bell.

Not teaching to the point of exhaustion.

Not leading solely through disruption. But cultivating cultures that support those who maintain them.

Leadership that safeguards identity.

Leadership that shares authority and responsibility. Leadership that weaves care into structure.

Leadership that sees partnership not as weakness, but as strength.

Leadership that endures beyond reform cycles, policy changes, and individual personalities.

Change is already underway.

The question is no longer whether education will continue to evolve. It will.

The question is whether leadership will keep handling pressure alone — or decide to redesign systems through disciplined partnership and shared responsibility.

That commitment is no longer aspirational.

It is the next responsibility.

# BEYOND BORDERS

## APPLYING EMOTIONAL LEADERSHIP ACROSS EDUCATION SYSTEMS

While the examples throughout this book mention specific countries and organizational contexts, the leadership framework it presents is not limited by geography. Emotional leadership, cultural adaptability, identity agility, and shared structural responsibility are not solely Western concepts. They are human leadership qualities that appear wherever individuals are asked to guide others through complexity, change, and growth.

Across continents, education systems face converging pressures: rapid reform cycles, workforce shortages, escalating student needs, technological acceleration, and rising expectations for equity and access. Whether leaders serve in public schools, private institutions, international networks, universities, NGOs, or government agencies, the core challenge remains the same—sustaining human capacity while advancing institutional progress.

The question isn't whether leadership needs to evolve globally. It already is. The more important question is how leadership is organized — and whether responsibility is shared or centralized.

This section provides a global view on applying the leadership principles outlined in this book across different education systems. It does not suggest one-size-fits-all solutions. Instead, it shows how emotionally grounded, culturally responsive, partnership-based leadership can be tailored to local contexts while keeping structural integrity and shared accountability.

## Sub-Saharan Africa

Education systems across Sub-Saharan Africa are undergoing rapid growth and change. Many countries are increasing enrollment, improving teacher training programs, upgrading infrastructure, and aligning national strategies with international goals like UNESCO's Sustainable Development Goal 4. At the same time, leaders often work within resource-limited environments characterized by high student-to-teacher ratios and shifting policy landscapes.

In these contexts, the sustainability of leadership becomes essential for the success of reform. When responsibility is concentrated in a few visible roles without emotional or structural support, turnover rises, and institutional momentum weakens. Emotional leadership offers more than relational strength; it provides a stabilizing infrastructure. By incorporating partnership into leadership development academies, ministry-sponsored cohorts, NGO initiatives, and teacher mentorship networks, responsibility can be shared rather than borne alone.

When collective care and shared authority are integrated into training systems, reform becomes more resilient and less reliant on individual endurance.

## Middle East and North Africa (MENA)

Across the Middle East and North Africa, education systems are rapidly modernizing. Investments in digital infrastructure, international curriculum integration, workforce strategies, and national reform agendas require leaders to manage multicultural teams, changing authority structures, and global accountability expectations.

In fast-paced environments, leadership identity often faces challenges. Leaders must balance tradition with innovation, national priorities with global standards, and institutional stability with rapid change. Emotional leadership supports this balance not by softening standards but by strengthening relational coherence.

Shared partnership becomes crucial in these situations. Reform cannot be achieved by positional authority alone. When leadership duties are shared among teams instead of being held at the top, the process becomes more stable and less disruptive. International school networks, higher education institutions, and ministry reform teams benefit most when leadership is organized as a collaborative effort rather than a centralized command.

## South and Southeast Asia

Education systems throughout South and Southeast Asia serve some of the world's largest and most diverse student populations. Leaders oversee multilingual classrooms, address rural–urban access gaps, implement large-scale policy initiatives, and develop national workforce strategies.

In large-scale systems, reform cannot rely solely on directive leadership. Policy doesn't implement itself. Lasting change requires relational trust, adaptability to context, and shared responsibility across all levels of leadership.

The approach described in this book encourages scalable reform by enhancing emotional regulation, collaborative decision-making, and partnership-based leadership structures. When leadership becomes a shared design process rather than a top-down directive, large systems maintain coherence even under pressure.

## Latin America

Across Latin America, education systems continue to face challenges related to equity, decentralization, institutional trust, and workforce stability. Leadership teams often operate at the crossroads of reform implementation, community rebuilding, and political transition.

In such environments, concentrated authority often increases fragility. When too much responsibility falls on a few leaders, systems become more susceptible to turnover and burnout.

Collective care and distributed leadership models provide structural protection. When mentorship programs, team-based decision-making processes, and relational accountability frameworks are integrated into institutional design, reform efforts become more sustainable. Leadership shifts from heroic endurance to coordinated partnership.

## Europe and North America

Education systems across Europe and North America face ongoing challenges: teacher attrition, leadership turnover, increased accountability demands, and post-pandemic workforce instability. Despite having relatively strong infrastructure, many leaders report emotional exhaustion, role overload, and declining sustainability.

In these settings, performance-focused cultures often prioritize outcomes but undervalue structural support. Emotional leadership redefines sustainability as intentional design rather than just a trait. By sharing emotional labor among teams and making partnership a key part of leadership, organizations can improve retention and maintain long-term health.

Shared responsibility here is more than just a philosophical choice; it's a strategic necessity.

## A Global Leadership Invitation

This book is written for leaders working across institutional and cultural boundaries. It is intended for public school systems, private education networks, colleges and universities, NGOs, ministry leadership programs, and international education organizations.

Wherever leaders are asked to stabilize change, protect people, and sustain learning, the principles in this book apply. But they are most effective when leadership moves from positional authority to structural partnership.

The future of education won't be determined by policy alone. It will be influenced by leaders who decide not just to withstand pressure, but to rethink how responsibility is distributed.

This is not regional leadership.

It is human leadership.

And it is needed everywhere.

As education systems keep evolving across borders and cultures, one question stays the same: what kind of leadership framework will we create in response?

It's not only about what kind of leaders we will become — but also how we will design systems that enable their endurance.

That question transcends geography.

It is structural.

# CONCLUSION

## THE NEXT GENERATION OF SCHOOL LEADERSHIP

The future of education will not be secured by leaders who simply endure.

For too long, leadership in schools and educational institutions has been defined by survival—the ability to withstand pressure, absorb dysfunction, and stay composed while systems strain under competing demands. This approach has created capable leaders but has also led to exhaustion, isolation, and the quiet erosion of professional purpose.

The next generation of school leadership requires something different.

It requires leaders who are emotionally anchored—grounded without becoming rigid, present without draining themselves. Emotional anchoring isn't about showing emotions or hiding them. It's about steadiness: an inner stability that helps leaders handle complexity without falling apart.

But steadiness alone is not enough.

The next generation of leadership must also be structurally aware and partnership-driven. It needs to go beyond individual resilience and move toward shared responsibility. Leaders should be able to look past individual performance and analyze the conditions shaping behavior, capacity, and culture. Burnout, disengagement, and resistance are rarely personal failures. They serve as signals—indicators that systems need redesigning.

Systemic awareness shifts leadership from blame to design. It redistributes responsibility instead of concentrating it. It redefines accountability as a shared structure rather than a personal burden.

This evolution also calls for leaders who are spiritually steady — not in a doctrinal sense, but in a way rooted in clarity of values and coherence of purpose. Spiritual steadiness enables leaders to act with integrity when certainty is limited, to lead with humility when control is incomplete, and to prioritize meaning over optics. It enhances the ability to balance urgency and patience, accountability and compassion, progress and care.

Throughout this book, leadership is redefined — not as control, charisma, or sacrifice, but as stewardship.

Stewardship recognizes that schools are not machines to be optimized but human systems to sustain. It understands that leadership impact is measured not only by the results achieved but also by the people retained, identities protected, and cultures strengthened over time. Stewardship dismisses the myth of the isolated leader and emphasizes that sustainable institutions are built through partnership.

The challenges in education are ongoing, not just short-term setbacks. Exhaustion from reform cycles, cultural complexities, identity stress, and emotional labor continue. Leadership models based on individual endurance will keep failing under these pressures — not because leaders lack skill, but because the expectations on them are inherently flawed.

The purpose of this book has never been to help leaders do more.

It has been to help them lead differently.

Embed emotional leadership into structure instead of personality. Distribute care rather than concentrating the burden. Create systems that protect people while pursuing purpose. Replace savior narratives with shared stewardship.

The next generation of school leadership is not heroic.

It is consistent. It is interconnected. It is structurally accountable.

Steady leaders do not dismiss emotion just to maintain momentum; they see it as valuable information. They do not confuse professionalism with hiding feelings; they demonstrate consistency. They do not lead alone; they build systems that can support many.

This type of leadership may not always grab headlines. It might not shine in crisis stories or quick-fix reforms. But it is the kind of leadership that helps institutions survive—not just practically but also on a human level.

Education doesn't need leaders who can endlessly manage flawed systems. It needs leaders prepared to redesign them.

The future depends on leaders who step forward not as saviors but as partners in shared responsibility — stewards of people, stewards of purpose, and stewards of institutions that must stay human to stay whole.

That is the work ahead.

And it is work that cannot — and should not — be done alone.

# THE WORK BEYOND THE BELL

## A LEADERSHIP RESET FOR SCHOOLS, EXECUTIVES, AND ORGANIZATIONS

### The 30-Day Emotional Leadership Reset

Leadership change does not begin with policy. It begins with presence.

If this book has made anything clear, it is that sustainability cannot be legislated into existence. It must be practiced. The next thirty days present an opportunity for recalibration—not through increased productivity, but through intentional design. This reset isn't about doing more; it's about leading with clarity, emotional steadiness, and structural awareness.

In the first week, concentrate on center awareness. Watch emotional patterns in your leadership setting without judgment. Recognize where you're absorbing stress that should be shared. Notice when you're reacting instead of discerning. Awareness is active, not passive; it helps identify issues. It reveals where emotional burdens are carried silently and where collaboration might be lacking.

In the second week, set boundaries that safeguard long-term capacity. This might include shortening meetings, clarifying agendas, minimizing reactive communication cycles, or clearly defining expectations. Boundaries are not restrictions; they serve as structural safeguards. They help prevent emotional labor from becoming invisible and unsustainable.

In the third week, concentrate on relational leadership. Initiate at least one conversation that focuses not on correction but on listening. Resist the urge to fix things immediately. Being present fosters trust more effectively than quick solutions. When leaders create space for shared reflection, they begin to share responsibility instead of bearing it all themselves.

In the fourth week, make one structural change to lower emotional strain within your system. Redesign a meeting format. Adjust communication protocols. Clarify who has decision-making authority. Redistribute leadership roles. Even small structural changes demonstrate that sustainability is a shared goal, not just an individual expectation.

Small adjustments, practiced regularly, create lasting momentum. Sustainable leadership seldom arises from dramatic changes; instead, it stems from consistent recalibration.

## Your First Three Leadership Moves

If you do nothing else after finishing this book, begin here.

First, enhance your leadership presence. Emotional stability isn't a luxury; it forms the foundation. Calm leadership promotes calm systems.

Second, recognize the emotional reality around you. What remains unspoken continues to affect behavior below the surface. What is acknowledged becomes easier to handle.

Third, modify a structural practice. Emotionally intelligent leadership must change how work is organized, not just how people manage within it. Partnership begins where responsibility is reassigned, and conditions are reviewed alongside expectations.

## Leadership Commitment Declaration

As you move forward, consider making a deliberate commitment — not to perfection, but to design.

I commit to leading with emotional integrity rather than emotional absorption.

I commit to fostering cultures of shared care and shared responsibility.

I commit to protecting people as intentionally as I pursue performance.

I commit to redesigning structures when strain becomes apparent. I commit to becoming the kind of leader this moment requires — not alone, but in partnership.

## Beyond the School Walls

### Emotional Leadership in Any System

This book began in schools for a reason.

Not because emotional leadership is unique to education. Not because educators experience more stress than leaders in other fields. But schools show signs of strain earlier than most institutions.

In schools, emotional labor is evident. It occurs in hallways, classrooms, parent meetings, faculty gatherings, and leadership offices. It shows up in student behavior, teacher exhaustion, principal changes, and the quiet adjustment of professional identities. Education systems operate amidst human complexity. When leadership structures break down, the cracks become more visible.

What happens in schools, however, does not stay in schools.

The emotional patterns discussed in this book—systemic exhaustion, leadership fatigue, resilience without relief, passive disengagement, silent resistance, toxic positivity, and identity erosion—are not limited to educational environments. They are structural leadership issues that are emerging across corporate businesses, nonprofit groups, healthcare systems, government agencies, and international companies with similar impact.

The terminology may shift.

The metrics may change.

The governance structures may differ.

But the emotional architecture is strikingly similar.

This chapter broadens the perspective. It remains focused on education. It shows how what is happening inside schools mirrors a larger leadership crisis emerging across different sectors.

## The Illusion of Sector-Specific Burnout

In corporate settings, burnout is often described using operational language—such as productivity drops, retention issues, engagement scores, and performance fluctuations. Leaders review dashboards, track quarterly results, and examine turnover trends. The discussion seems strategic and data-focused.

In education, burnout is more often described as fatigue, morale shifts, teacher attrition, principal resignations, and emotional overload. The language focuses on lived experience.

Yet when viewed clearly, the underlying dynamics reflect each other.

Standardized testing pressures resemble quarterly earnings expectations. District mandates mirror board directives. Initiative overload mirrors corporate restructuring cycles. Principal fatigue reflects executive burnout. Teacher disengagement mirrors quiet quitting.

In both contexts, leaders navigate extended instability while expected to display clarity, confidence, and composure. In both systems, emotional labor rises upward. In both cases, performance expectations grow while structural relief lags behind.

What is often called "education burnout" or "corporate burnout" is more accurately described as leadership system stress.

The difference is less about feeling exhausted and more about the words used to describe it. Education usually names emotional fatigue directly, while corporate systems often hide it with operational language. Beneath the surface, leaders in all sectors face the same reality: systems originally created for stability are being pushed to operate in ongoing volatility.

The question is no longer whether leaders can endure.

The question is whether endurance alone serves as a viable leadership strategy or if leadership architecture itself needs to evolve.

## Emotional Labor at the Executive Level

Corporate leadership carries its own form of emotional containment.

Executives are expected to exude confidence despite uncertainty, handle shareholder pressure without causing panic, manage political complexities across departments, lead culturally diverse teams, shape public perception while maintaining internal morale, and promote optimism amid structural challenges. These duties demand emotional control, relational insight, and a sense of stability that are often overlooked in traditional business training.

Like principals and superintendents, corporate leaders often serve as shock absorbers—buffering teams from instability while managing expectations from governing bodies. They interpret competing priorities, mediate tension, and bear responsibility for decisions shaped by forces they did not create and cannot fully control.

When emotional labor remains hidden, predictable consequences occur. Decision fatigue is mistaken for strategic detachment. Passive disengagement is seen as professionalism. Hesitancy to innovate is reinterpreted as prudent risk management. Leadership turnover is accepted as mobility rather than a sign of instability.

What is often missing is language.

The Mosaic Intelligence Method™ articulates what many leaders intuitively feel but cannot put into words: leadership is not solely based on authority. It requires emotional integrity—the ability to stay balanced without repression; cultural flexibility—the skill to manage differences without division; and identity agility—the capacity to adapt without losing oneself.

Without these capacities, leaders either become rigid or retreat. With them, they create stable environments without risking themselves.

But even these abilities cannot stay as individual traits. They need to be supported structurally.

## The Cost of Ignoring Emotional Architecture

Corporate systems often respond to exhaustion with efficiency solutions: workflow automation, productivity tools, incentive structures, motivational messaging, and optimization frameworks. These interventions may boost output temporarily, but they do not address misalignment in emotional architecture.

When leaders are forced to suppress their emotions without processing them, identity strain grows stronger. When teams face constant initiative stacking without adjusting capacity, disengagement quietly spreads. When cultures favor endurance over sustainability, high performers eventually withdraw or leave.

Neglecting emotional architecture results in shorter leadership tenures, cultural fragmentation, strategic inconsistency, a decline in innovation, and reputational vulnerability. Performance metrics may stay stable temporarily, but cultural instability eventually erodes long-term viability.

Emotional leadership is not a soft skill layered on top of operational strategy. It is a structural design.

Systems either intentionally distribute emotional labor through shared leadership structures or silently concentrate it at the top. When concentrated, costs build up until intervention becomes reactive instead of preventive. When distributed, resilience is built into the architecture rather than depending on heroic efforts.

Sustainable systems do not rely on exceptional endurance. They rely on intentional partnership.

## The Three Capacities Every Sector Now Requires

The leadership capacities outlined throughout this book are not confined to schools. They are cross-sector imperatives.

Emotional integrity in corporate settings appears as executive self-control during performance pressure, open accountability without performative apologies, strategic consistency amid volatility, and the courage to acknowledge stress without exaggerating it. Leaders lacking emotional integrity vacillate between urgency and withdrawal. Those who develop it foster environments of steady confidence.

Cultural flexibility in business settings requires cross-functional teamwork without territorial boundaries, understanding different generations, the ability to manage global teams across diverse values and norms, and adaptability during mergers and organizational changes. Without cultural flexibility, organizations tend to split into silos. With it, differences become a strategic advantage rather than a source of conflict.

Identity agility has become increasingly vital. Founders need to grow into scale leaders. Executives must adjust to technological disruptions. Professionals have to manage career pivots without losing their identity. Organizations must redefine roles during change. Rigidity in identity leads to fragility. Conversely, identity agility promotes sustainability.

These skills are not limited to educators. They characterize leadership maturity in any setting.

Yet they must be embedded into structure, not left to personality.

## Why Education Was the Right Starting Point

Education was the main focus of this book because it often shows broader leadership instability earlier and more clearly.

Schools function at the crossroads of social expectations, political pressures, economic disparities, generational conflicts, and technological changes. When leadership systems falter, education swiftly exposes the resulting effects.

In this sense, schools function as early indicators.

Teachers' emotional fatigue mirrors that of the workforce. Initiative overload in districts parallels corporate transformation cycles. Leadership turnover in schools reflects executive churn in the industry.

Examining emotional leadership through education offers clarity because the human impact is immediate and undeniable.

But the implications go far beyond school walls.

## A Cross-Sector Leadership Imperative

We are operating in an era marked by rapid technological change, workforce shifts, political division, global instability, and increased oversight. In this environment, leadership cannot depend solely on technical skills or operational power. Emotional intelligence has become vital for organizational survival.

Leaders who neglect emotional systems face cultural decline. Leaders who excessively absorb emotional strain risk losing their identity. Leaders who deliberately plan for sustainability ensure continuity.

Sustainable leadership now requires designing roles that protect human capacity, redistributing emotional labor through shared authority and collaborative accountability, aligning institutional values with operational realities, and fostering cultures where responsibility is structured rather than absorbed.

Whether within a school district, a multinational corporation, a nonprofit network, or a startup, the essential work remains the same: designing systems that do not demand constant emotional sacrifice to operate.

## An Invitation Beyond Education

If you lead in any capacity—whether in education, business, nonprofit, public service, or private enterprise—the invitation of this book extends to you.

Leadership is no longer measured by how much instability you can withstand. It is measured by how wisely instability is managed, how purposefully responsibility is organized, and how intentionally systems are built to safeguard the people within them.

It is not a test of endurance.

It is a test of architecture.

Leadership in this era demands partnership. It calls for leaders who are willing to go beyond formal authority and embrace shared responsibility—leaders who understand that sustainability results not from individual heroism but from collective effort.

It is defined by your commitment to emotional integrity under pressure, your practice of cultural flexibility in the face of difference, and your willingness to cultivate identity agility during periods of transition. However, it is supported by systems that collectively strengthen those abilities.

Beyond the school walls, the work continues.

The invitation remains the same:

Lead with emotional integrity so that clarity remains stable under pressure.

Lead with cultural flexibility so that differences become opportunities for design rather than sources of division. Lead with identity agility so that change enhances rather than diminishes your core. Lead through partnership so that responsibility builds strength instead of creating isolation.

Emotionally anchored.

Systemically aware.

Spiritually steady.

Structurally shared.

Not as aspiration.

As architecture.

And architecture, when created through shared responsibility and deliberate design, lasts.

# LEADERSHIP REFLECTION TOOLS AND FRAMEWORKS

This section translates the book's core arguments into disciplined leadership architecture.

It is designed to support individual leaders, leadership teams, and professional learning communities across K–12 and higher education settings—and increasingly across institutions facing similar structural challenges.

These are not quick fixes. They are reflective frameworks designed to slow leadership down enough to see clearly, respond intentionally, and redesign sustainably.

Each tool aligns with the four architectural capacities advanced throughout this book:

- Emotional integrity
- Cultural flexibility
- Identity agility
- Partnership as structural design

Partnership isn't just about collaboration. It's the deliberate sharing of responsibility, authority, emotional labor, and decision-making to ensure that sustainability doesn't rely on individual endurance.

Used consistently, these frameworks shift emotional leadership from personal disposition to institutional operating system. They move care from personality to structure. They transform steadiness from performance into shared architecture.

## 1. Reflection Prompts for Leaders and Leadership Teams

Reflection is not indulgence. It is infrastructure.

When leaders take a moment to analyze emotional patterns, authority flow, and structural gaps, they break cycles of quiet depletion before these become cultural norms. These prompts are intended for personal journaling, executive coaching, leadership retreats, and professional learning communities. They are meant to be revisited—not finished in a single session.

### Individual Leader Reflection

- Where am I absorbing emotional labor that should be redistributed through design?
- Which aspects of my leadership are grounded in integrity—and which are rooted in protection, performance, or fatigue?
- What am I stabilizing that the system itself has not been structured to support?
- Where am I defaulting to control instead of cultivating partnership?
- How is my leadership identity evolving—and where am I resisting that evolution?
- Where am I steady—and where am I compensating?

These questions cultivate emotional integrity by distinguishing between presence and overfunctioning.

### Leadership Team Reflection

- How is authority distributed across our leadership structure?
- Where is emotional labor quietly concentrated?
- Whose voices shape decisions—and whose perspectives remain peripheral?
- What tensions do we operationalize instead of relationally addressing?

- Where are we relying on resilience instead of redesign?
- If leadership were fully shared here, what would change structurally?

These prompts redirect the conversation from personality to architecture. Sustainability is not a stamina problem. It is a design decision.

## 2. Meeting Facilitation Guides for Partnership-Based Leadership

Meetings are not procedural events. They are cultural mirrors.

The way meetings are structured, facilitated, and concluded reveals how authority is exercised, how tension is handled, and how emotional labor is distributed.

Emotionally intelligent leadership requires partnership-based facilitation.

### Before the Meeting

- Clarify the meeting's function: decision, discernment, alignment, consultation, or redistribution of responsibility.
- Name authority boundaries explicitly to prevent performative input.
- Assess emotional readiness alongside logistical preparation.
- Identify where leadership might unintentionally default to centralization.

### During the Meeting

- Open by naming context and constraints—not just agenda.
- Normalize tension without dramatizing it.
- Separate emotional expression from directional clarity.
- Track who speaks, who hesitates, and who withdraws.
- Interrupt responsibility concentration when it emerges.

## After the Meeting

- Reflect on emotional residue in addition to deliverables.
- Follow up relationally where ambiguity lingers.
- Evaluate whether authority was shared or silently reclaimed.
- Ask whether the structure strengthened the partnership or reinforced the hierarchy.

When practiced consistently, meeting culture shifts from compliance management to shared leadership design.

## 3. Emotional Leadership Self-Assessments

These assessments are not performance measures. They are alignment indicators.

Leaders should revisit them periodically, not to score themselves, but to detect patterns of centralization, overextension, or fragmentation.

Patterns—not perfection—signal where redesign is necessary.

## Emotional Integrity

- I remain present under pressure without absorbing every emotional current.
- I hold boundaries without defensiveness or overjustification.
- I distinguish between empathy and over-responsibility.
- I recover from difficult moments without identity collapse.
- I name strain without dramatizing or minimizing it.

## Cultural Flexibility

- I pause interpretation before labeling resistance.
- I adjust communication without diluting standards.
- I recognize how identity, history, and context shape response.
- I distribute equity work rather than isolating a few.
- I remain curious longer than I remain certain.

## Identity Agility

- I can articulate how my leadership identity is evolving.
- I release outdated narratives that no longer serve the system.
- I tolerate ambiguity without defaulting to control.
- I remain coherent even as authority shifts.
- I adapt without dissolving.

## Partnership Capacity

- I share authority intentionally rather than reactively.
- I redistribute emotional labor instead of silently absorbing it.
- I design roles that protect collective capacity.
- I seek structural solutions before personal correction.
- I evaluate whether sustainability depends too heavily on me.

Partnership capacity is not optional. It is the stabilizing force that prevents emotional leadership from collapsing into solitary burden.

## 4. Case-Based Discussion Tools

*(Adaptable Across K–12, Higher Education, and Other Institutional Sectors)*

Case-based dialogue trains leaders to dissect complexity rather than default to evaluation.

These tools are effective in leadership academies, district cohorts, executive retreats, and cross-sector programs where structural strain must be addressed without personal exposure.

## Case Structure

Each case should include:

- Context: Institutional setting, power structures, resource constraints

- Tension: Emotional, cultural, or identity-based strain
- Decision Point: What must be redistributed, redesigned, clarified, or held

## Discussion Prompts

- What emotional architecture is visible here?
- Where is responsibility concentrated—and where should it be shared?
- What structural conditions are shaping behavior?
- What would partnership-based leadership redesign?
- How can accountability be maintained without isolating individuals?
- What systemic adjustment would prevent repetition?

These discussions train leaders to move from reactive judgment to structural discernment.

## Using These Tools Sustainably

These frameworks are most effective when they are:
- Embedded within existing leadership rhythms
- Practiced consistently rather than deployed in a crisis
- Modeled by senior leadership rather than delegated downward
- Paired with structural adjustment, where patterns emerge
- Treated as institutional commitments rather than personal improvement exercises

Reflection without redesign creates frustration.
Redesign without reflection creates repetition.
Sustainable leadership requires both.

## A Final Note on Practice

These tools do not simplify leadership. They deepen it.

When leaders reflect honestly, facilitate intentionally, assess humbly, and redistribute responsibility structurally, emotional leadership becomes operational rather than aspirational.

This is how cultures evolve.

This is how leadership transitions from endurance to architecture.

This is how institutions remain human without sacrificing rigor or performance.

*Beyond the Bell: Reclaiming Emotional Leadership in Schools* is not a motivational supplement. It is not compliance training. It is not ideology.

It is a structural leadership framework.

It integrates theory, lived experience, and institutional design. It challenges leaders not to carry more—but to redesign how leadership is shared.

The work does not end here.

This section exists so the work continues—

not through isolated effort,

but through intentional partnership.

Steadily.

Structurally.

Together.

## Institutional Applications and Leadership Development Integration

### District Leadership Development

For districts, *Beyond the Bell* provides more than a common language—it offers structural recalibration.

Instead of seeing burnout, resistance, and disengagement as just personnel issues, this framework views them as systemic signals. It urges district leaders to examine how authority is distributed, how emotional labor is handled, and where structural changes are needed to protect capacity.

Districts can deploy this book as:

- A core text for superintendent-led leadership academies
- A framework for aligning policy, principal support, and culture strategy
- A reflective anchor during consolidation, reform cycles, or leadership transition
- A shared language for redistributing responsibility rather than concentrating it

Its focus on emotional integrity, cultural flexibility, identity agility, and partnership as structural design makes it especially relevant for districts navigating post-crisis fatigue, equity implementation, or recurring leadership turnover.

When used systemically—not symbolically—it strengthens leadership coherence across levels.

## Principal Preparation Programs

Principal and assistant principal preparation programs often focus on compliance, operations, and instructional systems. What they rarely directly address is the emotional and identity complexity of leadership authority.

*Beyond the Bell* prepares emerging leaders for what is always experienced but seldom taught:

- Emotional labor and relational strain
- Identity expansion as authority increases
- Boundary-setting without detachment
- Partnership-based leadership rather than positional control
- Sustainable steadiness under persistent pressure

Programs can incorporate the text into coursework, cohort discussions, case-based analyses, and capstone reflections to ensure that future leaders not only are technically prepared but also understand the structural aspects of their roles.

The goal is not just to create resilient individuals, but also to develop leaders who can design shared leadership systems from the beginning.

## University Education Departments

Within colleges of education, this book serves as a bridge between research, leadership theory, and institutional practice.

It strengthens coursework in:

- Educational leadership and administration
- Organizational behavior
- Change management
- Policy implementation under complexity

By applying a human-systems perspective, it broadens administrative preparation to include emotional frameworks and structural collaboration.

Its applicability across K–12 and higher education settings supports cross-sector dialogue without diminishing contextual differences. This makes it suitable for graduate seminars, Ed.D. cohorts, and faculty-led inquiry exploring leadership in volatile environments.

## Leadership Coaching Cohorts

*Beyond the Bell* serves as an anchor framework for leadership coaching cohorts and professional learning communities.

Its reflective architecture and partnership emphasis support:

- Executive coaching programs
- Peer leadership cohorts
- Principal, dean, and department chair coaching structures
- Cross-functional leadership development initiatives

The integration of identity agility and emotional anchoring naturally aligns with coaching methods focused on awareness and integration. At the same time, the structural focus ensures coaching conversations go beyond personal coping and into organizational redesign.

Coaching grounded in this framework does not simply build self-awareness. It strengthens shared accountability.

## Faculty Resilience and Retention Initiatives

For institutions tackling faculty burnout and attrition, this book shifts the resilience discussion from endurance to shared responsibility.

It is particularly relevant in initiatives focused on:
- Faculty burnout and retention strategy
- Role overload and professional isolation
- Leadership–faculty trust repair
- Mentorship and succession design

Instead of only expecting resilience from faculty, Beyond the Bell empowers leaders to redesign the conditions that foster engagement and belonging.

Sustainability becomes architectural rather than aspirational.

## Why This Book Stands Apart

This book occupies a distinct position in the leadership landscape because it:
- Treats emotional leadership as infrastructure rather than personality
- Frames partnership as a structural distribution of responsibility.
- Integrates identity, culture, and system design cohesively
- Speaks to leaders without romanticizing sacrifice
- Applies across K–12 and higher education without flattening nuance
- Bridges emotional intelligence and institutional architecture

It offers depth without dogma.

Reflection without abstraction.

Recalibration without ideology.

Most importantly, it reframes sustainability not as individual stamina, but as shared design.

## Strategic Summary

*Beyond the Bell* is not positioned as a temporary response to burnout. It is a durable leadership framework for institutions committed to coherence, sustainability, and human-centered systems.

It is best integrated as:

- A core leadership development text
- A cohort-based reflection and training resource
- A superintendent- or dean-level recalibration tool
- A policy-adjacent framework for cultural redesign
- A bridge between emotional intelligence and structural partnership

In a moment when education continues to ask leaders to carry more than ever, this book offers something rare:

Not another demand.

But a different design.

A leadership model that redistributes strain, protects identity, strengthens culture, and sustains institutions over time.

# BRIDGE TO *LEAD ANYWAY*

*Beyond the Bell* names the emotional truth of leadership in today's schools.

*Lead Anyway* shows what to do next.

Where *Beyond the Bell* emphasizes systems, culture, and sustainability, 'Lead Anyway' shifts focus inward, addressing the daily, lived experiences of educators and leaders who are asked to keep showing up even when the system no longer sees them clearly.

*Lead Anyway* is a companion, not a repetition.

It speaks directly to:

- Educators navigating emotional fatigue and identity fragmentation
- Leaders holding responsibility without adequate support
- Professionals who still care deeply—but are tired of pretending they are fine

While *Beyond the Bell* reframes leadership as collective, structural, and systemically aware, *Lead Anyway* meets the individual educator at the moment of doubt and asks a different question:

How do you maintain integrity in leadership when conditions are unclear, recognition is inconsistent, and the cost feels personal?

## Why *Lead Anyway* Comes Next

Readers who finish Beyond the Bell often see themselves in its pages—particularly the emotional weight, cultural tension, and leadership strain it highlights. Lead Anyway builds on that recognition and offers:

- Language for emotional exhaustion without shame
- Validation of identity strain without collapse
- Grounded leadership practices for moments when clarity is missing
- A reminder that leadership is not revoked by fatigue

It is especially powerful for:

- Teachers who feel invisible but still influential
- Leaders who no longer identify with traditional authority models
- Educators carrying emotional labor without institutional backing

## The Throughline

*Beyond the Bell* asks leaders to redesign systems.
*Lead Anyway* reminds educators why they still matter within them.
Together, these books form a complete leadership arc:

- One addresses how schools must change
- The other addresses how educators survive—and lead—while that change unfolds

For readers who finished *Beyond the Bell* feeling seen, challenged, and reflective, *Lead Anyway* offers a steady next step:
Not louder leadership.
Not harder leadership.
But leadership that continues—
with integrity, clarity, and self-respect.
**Lead anyway.**

# ABOUT THE AUTHOR

Dr. Karissa Thomas is an educational leadership scholar, practitioner, and award-winning author whose work focuses on sustainable system design, emotionally intelligent leadership, and identity development in complex institutional environments.

With professional experience across K–12 education, higher education, and executive leadership development, Dr. Thomas offers a unique blend of academic rigor and hands-on leadership practice in her writing. Her research examines how leaders navigate emotional labor, cultural complexities, increasing authority, and identity challenges—especially within systems under ongoing pressure and reform.

She is the creator of the Mosaic Intelligence Method™, a leadership framework built on four core capacities: emotional integrity, cultural flexibility, identity agility, and partnership as structural design. Through this framework, Dr. Thomas redefines leadership sustainability as a shared institutional responsibility rather than a personal endurance test. Her work challenges traditional models that reward overfunctioning and silent sacrifice, instead promoting a structural approach that redistributes emotional labor, aligns authority with accountability, and protects human capacity while upholding organizational rigor.

Her books are used in district leadership academies, principal preparation programs, university education departments, executive coaching cohorts, and institutional recalibration initiatives that seek depth without dogma and clarity without abstraction.

Known for a voice that is grounded yet intellectually precise, Dr. Thomas provides leaders with language for experiences they often bear alone—while equipping them with frameworks that make those burdens shareable and structurally supported.

She continues to collaborate with educators, institutions, and leadership teams dedicated to fostering cultures of coherence, sustainability, and shared stewardship—where leadership is not heroic or performative, but steady, distributed, and designed to last.